BROKEN

Tiffini Johnson

Thank You

To Breathe and Alight, for shining joy into the places of shadow and defining hope where once there was none. Being your Mama is the most important thing I have ever done. I love you both to the moon, around the world and back!

Also, to God, for holding my hand, for never walking away and for all the healing stories that have filled my head, heart and paper for as long as I can remember... thank You. To You, may all the glory go.

To my Mama, Vicki, for inspiring all that may be good within me, for being my best friend and for loving me unconditionally. I love you with all my heart!

And finally,

To my sister, Mandi, for inspiring in me a passion for life and for laughing for no reason with me ever since we were babies, I love you. Also, thank you for your invaluable help with key parts in this book! One day, I still hope to be just like you!

This story is the first person account of a troubled teenage girl.

There are many things in this novel that could act as potential triggers to anyone suffering from suicidal thoughts, self-destructive behaviors or whose history includes abuse of any kind. Your physical and emotional well-being is more important to the author than your reading this book.

Please make sure you are safe before reading.

I have to write this letter to you. If you're reading this, then it means you found me. I've put towels on the floor and have tried real hard to keep it as clean as I can. I know it was still shocking and probably scary to find me, though. I'm sorry about that. If I could do it so nobody would ever know what happened to me, I would. But I don't want anyone worrying about me, wondering where I am or anything like that. Mom needs to know I haven't run away; she needs to know what happened to me. So there was no way to avoid the mess.

Mom's the only one who has ever really loved me. And she's the only one I've ever really, really loved. If it weren't for her, I'd have done this a very long time ago.

Mom told me to be strong. She told me to have courage. But I can't anymore. Staying alive is too hard, it takes too much courage. You have to get up, hoping for a good day, but in your heart of hearts, you just know that it's *going to be a day just like every day before. Mom told me to have courage. Staying alive is brave because, if you're alive, you have to keep trusting people. You have to trust them not to hurt you. You have to trust them to tell you the truth. You have to trust them to take care of you. But nobody does that. Nobody tells the truth anymore, nobody wants to take care of me and I'm just not strong enough to take care of myself. I don't want to. It hurts too much.*

I've thought of Mom a lot lately. Ever since I realized there was no other way than this, I been thinking about her. I remember when I was a little girl how she'd tuck me in every night. Sometimes when she thought I was asleep, she would come in my room, put oil on my forehead and pray. Sometimes she would pray out loud. She always asked God to protect me.

I don't know what I think about God. It would be nice to think I'm going to Heaven. When I was a little girl, I remember walking down the aisle at church in front of everybody to get saved. A preacher, Brother James, put his hand on my head, made me recite a prayer after him, and hugged me. He told me I was for sure going to Heaven. I was saved.

But that was before.

Before I got bad. I mean, I hadn't done anything too bad at that point. I really was a pretty good girl all my life up til then. I obeyed my mom and my dad. And I didn't try to get away with anything too stupid. I didn't say bad words just to say them or anything. I said my prayers ever night too. I don't think there would have been too many reasons to keep me out of Heaven then. But then I turned bad. Bad things started happening at nighttime, and I didn't say nothing about it. I mean, it wasn't that big a deal; it wasn't like I was being beat or nothing. I didn't have bruises on me. At least not any that anybody could see. It wasn't as bad as it could have been, but it made me feel weird. It kept me from having any friends.

And friends is what I've wanted most of my life.

I thought I had them one night. One night, I thought I was part of a group. I thought I fit in. We laughed. I thought we were having fun. Really, they were just laughing at me. But I didn't know that then. Once, I thought I had some friends. I thought I was normal. Maybe I thought that because I wanted friends so much. I wanted to fit in. I wanted them to like me. So I

*did stupid stuff, stupid stuff I knew I shouldn't
have been doing.*

And they laughed at me.

*I just wanted someone to talk to me. I
just wanted someone to care. Nobody did. I'm
just a freak. It's all over me. I've got cuts all
over me. Nobody else has cuts on them. But I
do. Last week, I carved the word FREAK on my
right arm. I carved it so deep it's there forever
now. It's like a tattoo. There ain't no point in
denying what you really are. If you are
something, you might as well own it. And I am a
freak. Everybody at school knows it. Dad
knows it.*

*Anyway. I don't know if God is real
anymore. I don't know how He can be. It seems
like if He were, He wouldn't put up with all the
crap that goes on down here. It seems like He
would stop it right quick when good people got a
shitty hand dealt them. The bullies are heroes,
and their victims are freaks. Does that sound
like something the God of the Bible would be ok
with? I don't know. I hope Heaven is real,
though. And, Mom, don't worry, I asked Him
for forgiveness for what I done tonight, so, if
there is a Heaven, maybe He'll let me in. I hope
there is one. Even if there ain't, though, or even*

if I go to Hell for what I'm doing, it's better than being hated or ignored here every day and messed with every night. And, with Dad coming home, this is the only way for me to be free.

I'm not doing this just because I'm bored. Or because I want attention. Or maybe I am. Maybe that's right, what they say about my kind. Maybe that is what we want, after all. I mean, if I had a real friend, even just one, maybe I would have a good reason not to do it. But I don't think it's because I want attention. Mom always said, "You only fight after you've tried every other way." I've tried everything. I've tried so hard. Nothing has worked. So this has to.

I'm doing it because my whole life is ruined. Nobody is ever going to see me as anything else anymore. I'm doing it because nobody is ever going to want to be my friend. I'm doing it because I can't get the bugs off of me, just like I can't get the scars off my arms. I'm doing it because I'm tired of waking up crying every night. I'm doing it because I'm tired of being scared of the dark. I'm doing it because, even if I turned eighteen and moved out, nobody would ever love me if I didn't do it for him a lot, but even once is a lot, and I just

*can't handle it. It wouldn't be real love,
because if I was tired one night or sick or just
didn't feel like it, he wouldn't love me anymore
either.*

*Mom tells me think of my future. She
used to say that whenever I got sad, I should
think about all the things I had to look forward
to. Maybe I would have been a teacher. That's
what I wanted to be, when I was little. I
remember getting paper and writing addition
and subtraction problems for my baby dolls to
practice. I taught them. And I've always done
real good in school. Other kids, even the
popular ones, would say tests were hard, but I
never thought they were. I always made straight
A's, so I think I could have made a good teacher.*

*Except that nobody would let me teach
their kids, cause I've got scars on my arms and
besides, I'd only mess it up like I messed up the
game. I'd probably scare the kids, or pass
somebody that couldn't even read. And the first
time I ever saw a student bully another student,
I'd fail him for the whole year even if he got real
good grades on the tests. Yeah, I wouldn't make
a good teacher after all. You have to be normal
to have that kind of job. I'd probably end up a
waitress or something like that. Besides, it don't*

matter. None of it matters if you're not loved and nobody loves me. Nick said he never loved me even a little, even though he told me he did. He was just lying, I guess. Cause everybody lies. And you can't be happy if nobody loves you. If you're just one of those people, like me, that is never going to get somebody to love you, then why bother being strong? What does it matter if you're brave, if nobody can stand being in the same room as you? He said I was ugly. He called me a freak, and everybody else did too. They said I was trash. And I know they're right because Dad thinks the same thing. He told me so. How could you ever possibly be good if your own dad thinks you're trash? Why even try? Mom used to sing me a song every night that said, "This little light of mine, I'm going to let it shine." But what are you supposed to do when you don't have a light at all?

So you understand, right, why I have to do this? You understand that there really is no other way for me. I just wasn't ever as strong or as brave as everybody else. I was never really meant to be here. When Mom told Dad that she was pregnant with me, he cried, he was so sad. That's what he told me. I was a mistake right from the start. I'm just trying to erase the mistake, that's all.

But I want Mom to know that it's not her fault. She did everything she could for me. She prayed. She made me go to school, even if I didn't want to. She used to play peek-a-boo with me when I was a baby, for crying out loud. I know because I saw the pictures of her doing it. And she wasn't afraid to hug me. I don't want her to think I don't remember all the good things she did for me. I don't want her to think none of those things matter to me, because they all do. She was a really good mother. She's probably the only one who will cry at my funeral. But I don't want her to. I don't even really want a funeral at all. What I wish is that I could just be burned and have my ashes thrown out to the sea. I don't like the idea of being in the ground. I've always been real scared of the dark. But it don't matter, I won't really be there, right?

One more thing has to be said.

Maybe no one knows, Dad. Maybe no one ever will. And maybe it wasn't that big a deal. I'm sure lots of kids have it worse than I ever did, just like you said. Maybe no one will ever know all the things you did, or made me do. Maybe no one will ever know all the things you

said, even when you didn't say anything at all.
Maybe no judge will ever send you to jail for it.
Maybe you'll live to be a very, very old man who
always drinks coffee without cream and two
things of sugar every morning. Maybe you'll
never feel a need to tell anybody about me.
Maybe you'll forget all about it. I don't know.
No matter what else happens, though, I want you
to know one thing: you are the real reason I'm
dead. In fact, I really died a long time ago,
when I was just nine years old, didn't I? At
least, most of me did. And no matter what else
happens, now you'll know that, and maybe
you'll remember it every time I'm not there for
you to touch.

     So then.
     It's time.
     Mom, I love you. Please forgive me.

     Goodbye,
     Taya

Most mornings, when I wake up, I don't know what town I'm in. I don't know what state I'm in. Sometimes it takes me a minute to remember the layout of the particular house I'm in. Today is no different. I smell biscuits in the oven, and bacon. I blink, and then look to the side, at the walls. They are painted cobalt blue. Posters of Pink and a WARNING! DO NOT ENTER! sign hangs on my door. That's when memory starts to come back to me. It takes only a second for me to remember that we're in Baton Rouge, Louisiana right now. We've been here a couple months, ever since the police almost trapped Dad for getting a couple computers under a fake business name and never paying for them. It's like a never ending game of cat and mouse we play. When the cops get too close, we run somewhere new.

It's Saturday, so I don't have to go to school. It's a really small school, and they are weird there. Grades sixth, seventh and eighth sit in this big room. Each kid has a cubicle, and workbooks. We do the work in our workbooks and if we need help, we have an American flag that we put up on the top of our cubicle to get a teacher over to us. There is no lecture. There isn't really what you think of as "class." It's very odd. But I don't have to worry about that. We won't be here long. We are never anywhere long. It's almost summer, and this is already my third school of the year.

The smell of bacon makes me get up. I run a hand through my hair and shuffle downstairs. I pass Dad in the living room, talking on the phone. I don't know who he's talking to, but I can tell from the tone of his voice that he's at it again. When he gets off the phone, he'll be in a hurry, saying he has to go meet some guy about a job. He'll come home later this afternoon with money he didn't really earn but that we can use to buy groceries and pay the rent for a few months.

I pass him and go into the kitchen.

Mom's putting bacon on a plate. She knows it is my favorite.

"Hey," she says.

"Hi." I open the fridge and pull out the orange juice. I open the top and take a drink out of the carton. Mom doesn't say anything. Instead, she stays busy by cleaning the mess up from cooking, putting the dishes in the dishwater and the extra food in Tupperware. Mom never eats breakfast. I think she cooks breakfast not really so that I'll eat but because it makes her feel like everything is normal.

Nothing is normal in my house.

Dad walks in and grabs his coat from the back of one of the chairs. He doesn't even see me but goes straight to Mom. "I've got to meet with up with them today, in an hour. I'll be back in a little while." He kisses her, then turns. I'm sitting right in front of him, but it's like I'm invisible. He doesn't say anything, passes me right on by. Mom follows him, telling him a list of things we need to buy. Groceries, mainly.

"Goodbye, Dad," I mumble sarcastically, looking down at my bacon. I bite off a piece. A minute later, I hear Mom go into the bedroom and close the door.

I put my plate in the sink, then look out the back door. The sun is shining brightly. It's a great day for a walk. I change into my jeans and a faded pink shirt then slip on flip flops. I tell Mom I'm going out, just so she doesn't start yelling my name out the front door, then head outside.

I like this place.

The trees are really green here, and this is a nice neighborhood. My family, we're like pretenders. We always get a nice house, and a nice car. We always have *things*. Except the things that really matter, like a home that's really ours. Friends.

Behind the last house of the cul-de-sac we live on are some woods. I probably shouldn't cut behind their house to walk into the woods, but I do. I know deer live in the woods because I've seen them. It's like my own little hideaway. When I'm around other people, even my own family, I feel like I'm wearing a mask. It's like I'm holding my breath, when I'm around others, always looking around for the next bomb to drop. Being around others is like having my insides shaken up, all the time.

Until they all go away.

Only when I'm by myself do I get to breathe. Only when I'm by myself does the shaking inside me stop. It's a freeing feeling. And that's why I go into these woods. When we move, I'm going to miss them.

I find a tree and sit down against it. The bark feels rough against my back, the grass-covered ground soft against my legs that I've got stretched out in front of me. I lean my head back against the tree and close my eyes.

The breeze blowing through the trees, that's what I'm thinking about. It sounds like music. The sun is blocked by a canopy of leaves high above me but a few bright rays still break through, hitting me on the face. I hear grass whistling around me and wonder what caused it. Did an acorn fall out of one of the trees? Did a squirrel race by? A deer?

Hours pass, but I don't care. I've moved around some. I got up and walked a little deeper into the woods. I'm looking for treasures now. Did you ever play that game when you were a kid? Treasure hunting? I didn't.... but I play it now. I'm looking for neat or unusual rocks. I've got a collection of rocks in my room. Sometimes I like to line them out, one by one, and make up stories about them in my head. I used to paint them but I haven't done that in a long time now.

I see an oval shaped rock that's pretty big and it's very smooth. It's got an unusual, coral tint color. I pick it up and then my stomach growls. It's probably about time for lunch. Mom may be wondering where I'm at. I pull the bottom of my shirt up and drop the rocks I've gathered in it, kind of like a sack, and head for home.

I hear it before I see it.

Mom is screaming.

I don't hear Dad, but that's because he usually doesn't scream. He just attacks. The breath gets lodged in my throat. Part of me wants to hide back in the woods. I'm not going to do any good by going home. But I know I can't now. I can't just run away. Somebody might get hurt. If they see me, maybe they'll stop.

I don't walk fast though.

I can't hear what they are saying; I can only make out the screaming. I see Mom pick up a rock and throw it at Dad. Now, I'm closer and I can see better. Dad's trying to get in the car. He pushes Mom down to the ground, but she gets back up and grabs his arm. "You are *not* leaving again! No!"

Dad's in the car now anyway but Mom's not letting him shut the door. I know why. She's scared. She's scared that if he drives away, he won't come back. I know there's nothing I can do. I cut through between two houses and into our back yard. I go in the back door and up to my room. A minute later, I hear the front door slam shut and the voices are louder.

Dad's still here.

Mom won.

That makes my heart hurt just a little. I know I shouldn't but, sometimes, a little piece of me wishes he would just drive off and we'd never hear from him again. Mom thinks it would make life harder. I think it would make life easier.

Somebody crashed into a wall. I hear Dad screaming now too. Something breaks. My heart races in my chest. I hate hearing sounds like this without being able to see what's causing it. It makes me think somebody might be getting hurt. But I don't want to see.

I reach over and grab my headphones. I put them on and turn the music on. Even with the music on loud, I can hear the fighting. I don't know what started the fight but I know it's probably about whatever Dad brought home, or didn't, from the meeting. It's probably about money.

When the song goes off, I pull one side off my ear. The noise is still going strong. The music isn't helping. I don't take the headphones off, though. I just reach over and grab the remote to the TV in my room. I turn it on and flip the channels until a black and white show catches my eye. I stop it. Andy Griffith's walking down a lane and a little boy is beside him. They're going fishing. I turn the volume up and stare at the screen. I have no idea what's happening on the show because I've got the earphones on too. But the TV and the headphones together do the trick. I can't hear the fighting downstairs.

Now, the little freckle faced kid is sitting on his dad's knee. His dad looks stern.... But friendly. The freckle faced kid gives him a hug. Something pierces my heart, hurts it bad. I jerk my eyes away from the screen as a commercial comes on. I never sat in my dad's lap like that. Not when I was little and definitely not after I turned nine. I don't a hug from him, either, and haven't since I don't know when.

The show comes back on.

The dad is talking to a gangly officer. I can't help what they're saying but I know it's funny. Then Andy's out walking the neighborhood and he nods to everybody. Says hi. I feel my heart squeeze tight again. Everybody knows everybody in Mayberry. And everybody loves everybody. There are no drop down, drag out fights between parents in Mayberry.

I watch the rest of the show. I never hear a word of what's being said, but somehow I know whatever's wrong will be okay. I pull one side of the headphones off my ears again. I hear the TV and I hear screaming. I put the headphone back on. I don't know why, but tears burn the backs of my eyes.

By the time Andy Griffith goes off, the yelling downstairs has finally stopped. I have a headache from the music being so loud in my ears for so long, though. I turn the television off and lay down on my bed. I wonder where everybody is.

My stomach is still grumbling. I am still hungry. I get up and try to make as little noise as possible as I open the bedroom door. I creep downstairs. Dad is sitting on the couch, knees spread apart, one hand cupping the other as if it's hurt. I bet it is. He looks up at me but doesn't say anything as I walk past him into the kitchen. I don't see Mom. She's probably in the bedroom.

I get a bologna sandwich with
mayonnaise and then grab four big Dorito chips,
lay them on top of the bologna. I take the bread,
put it on the sandwich and smash it in, until the
chips break into smaller pieces. Bologna and
Dorito chip sandwiches are my favorite.

***** ****** *****

It's late.

I don't know how late it is but the world
outside is black. I'm lying on the bed, staring
out the window. The later it gets at night, the
blacker it gets. And still. You can tell when it's
really late at night because it gets real still-like
outside. Tears still drip from the edges of my
eyes. Dad just left the room a few minutes ago.
I don't know why I still cry. It's weird. I'm
usually okay until he kisses me. But for some
reason, when he kisses me, it's like a dam bursts.
I also know when he's mad and when he's just
bored. When he's mad, he grabs my jaw
between his fingers while he's pounding away
so that I can't look away from him.

It's funny.

People think you'd, you know, never get
used to it. But you do. You can get used to
anything, if it happens enough. I can even tell
how long it's going to last by the way he gets it

started. If he comes in and asks how my day went, he's not mad, he's just bored, so it'll last longer. If he comes in, like tonight, though, asking me where the hell I went off to all day... he's mad. These nights don't last as long, but they're worse. These are the nights he calls me names. I can't tell you how many times I've heard the word "trash." I've even gotten used to that. I've gotten used to everything but the kissing. That still makes me cry.

I roll over and curl my legs up. I am naked and usually I'd care about that. Usually, I'd get dressed. Right now, though, I don't care at all. I wrap my arms around my waist and bend my head in to my chest as far as it will go.

I'll tell.

The thought comes out of nowhere. It comes every time. *I'll tell*, the tantalizing idea that haunts me. I wouldn't even really *have* to tell. I could just start screaming one night, I could just scream so loud Mom would wake up. She'd run up the stairs to see what's wrong and when she found the door locked, I'd yell *help, get him out of here*.

I'm pretty sure she would bust down the door.

I'll tell.

Except that I really won't.

Because then it would just be me and Mom. Mom's family lives in another state, a long way away in Colorado. And they're just a little bit crazy. When she's not fighting with Dad, she's usually fighting with at least one person from her family. They wouldn't help us. We'd be evicted from this house in no time flat. Dad would have taken the car to another country by then and we would be stranded here with no money, no job, no family, no nothing. Sure, eventually, we'd get a job…. Get a house. But… what would we do until then?

In my head, I see a picture of the show I watched earlier. I see Andy Griffith smiling and walking down a dirt road with his son. If I lived in Mayberry, I could tell. There would be a sheriff who would promise my mom and me everything would be ok. He'd take my dad to jail. He'd know somebody who would let Mom work. Until we got on our feet, he'd let us stay at his house. Aunt Bee would fix us dinner every night. And that's the way it would be because on TV right from wrong is black and white, not gray. Neighbors are friends, not strangers. And everybody looks out for one another. On the show. But not in real life. In real life, nobody knows anything about a neighbor's family. And they wouldn't really bring us dinner every night and give us hugs.

If I lived in Mayberry, I wouldn't have to worry about hurting Mom. I could know to trust the sheriff because I would have known him all my life, ever since I was little baby, and I could just tell him what happened tonight. He would tell my mom for me, so that I wouldn't have to. We wouldn't be stranded; we'd be surrounded by safety and neighbors who were friends. I wouldn't cry at night because I'd know for sure that things would be better in the morning.

If I lived in Mayberry.

But I don't. When I wake up in the morning, I won't even know what town I'm in at first. And, in my closet, two boxes are still packed. There's no point in getting everything out. I'd just have to pack them again soon. This way, when they tell me it's time to go, I can just throw those boxes in the car and then pack what I have to have every day like my clothes and toothpaste.

I'm starting to get a little cold.

My body aches, especially inside my vagina. It feels really sore. I stretch out my legs, trying to get the soreness gone, and roll to my back. My nose is stuffy, and my eyes are swollen. I breathe out slowly through my mouth and use the back of my hand to wipe the tears that are falling from my eyes away. Because I don't live in Mayberry.

"Taya, Taya, wake up." It is my mom.

She is shaking me awake. It is late at night, but I don't know how late. I sit up. My mom is fully dressed, not in her pajamas, but in a pair of jeans a sweater. Her hair is pulled back into a ponytail and her face looks worried, and serious. She doesn't have any makeup on. I hear Dad call from downstairs, asking if we are ready. He has only been home from jail about a month and already, this again. My mom is at my dresser now, throwing my clothes into a suitcase. She tosses me my heart shaped pink pillow and tells me that I don't have to get dressed; we can stop at a rest area later and change. Right now, it's just time to go.

Then, like the wind, she's out of the room again and it's just me. I am not really awake yet, still half asleep. I roll out of bed, grab my purse and the blanket off my bed by the corner, then trudge downstairs. The front door is open, and I can hear the engine of the car running already. The house looks bare, except for the furniture. We will leave it behind. There are bags by the front door and Dad is throwing them into the trunk of the car. I can tell they are in a hurry, but I go slowly into the kitchen, open the fridge and take out the only thing in it: one last can of Coke. Then I walk out the front door, get into the backseat and slam the car door behind me. There are pillows thrown in the floorboard. I grab one, pull it up to the seat and then lay down, crunched up on my side, and pull the blanket over me. I shut my eyes and pray for sleep.

A few minutes later, Mom opens the door and gets in. "Taya, did you get everything?" She asks. She's asking me if I got everything that matters from my room. Since nothing really matters, I don't answer. Before she can ask me again, the driver's side door opens and Dad slides in. He and Mom start talking in low voices. I pretend I don't hear them. I want to go to sleep again, but I can't. So I sit up and stare out the window. Dad is backing out of the driveway. The house with the pretty front porch and white shutters stares back at me. The yard needs cutting, I think to myself. The yard in all

the houses we've ever lived in needs cutting.
Dad drives along the street now, and I watch as
one house after another slips away. I don't
know any of our neighbors, but I have seen their
faces for a year. We have lived in this house for
a year. That's 365 days. That's a long time.
We've never lived in a house that long. I even
know shortcuts around the neighborhood. Like,
if you turn down Appleton Street, you still come
out at Trousdale, the big four lane road, but you
don't have to go through all the stop lights. Just
two stop signs instead. I've never known
shortcuts anywhere else we've ever lived. I don't
think about the school until we pass it. John C.
Baker High School. It is where I started high
school just a month ago. I wonder where I will
finish high school. It won't be wherever we are
headed to now, that much I know. I think about
the teachers at John C. Baker. Mrs. Yager and
Mrs. Huntsville. They are nice. Mrs. Yager
even stayed after school one day to help me
study for the math test last week because I hate
math. I failed it, but she knew how hard I tried
so she let me take the same test a second time.
No one else got to do that. She is a good
teacher. I wonder what she will think when I
don't come to school tomorrow. Or the next

day. Or the day after that. Maybe I can write her a letter and explain.

We're finally on the interstate now. But it is so late at night that there aren't any cars on the road with us. We pass a big bread company semi-truck. I think about when I was young, how I would roll my fingers into a fist and then pull my arm straight down and straight up, like I was pulling a horn, every time we passed a semi-truck. Some of the nicer ones will honk at you when they see you do that. Mom and Dad have stopped talking now. Everything is quiet, except the engine and the air conditioner. I roll over, laying down, again and close my eyes. If I stay like this long enough, I will go to sleep.

I don't know how long we drive. But when I feel the vibrating of the car stop and open my eyes, the sky outside is purplish with hints of pink in it. It is almost morning. We drove all night long. I sit up and look out of the window. There is a Quality Inn staring back at me. I have no idea what city we are in. But I know what the inside of the hotel looks like. We have stayed at more of them than we have houses. Dad goes in to rent the room. Mom looks back at me and smiles. "Are you hungry?" She asks.

I shake my head, still staring outside at the

hotel's sign. I look around and see the Hampton across the street. The Hampton is nicer than the Quality Inn. Their breakfast is better, and the rooms are bigger. We stayed at one Hampton Inn that actually had two rooms together. There was a couch and everything, kind of like a living room, and then a bedroom with a door. Mom and Dad let me have the bedroom, and they slept on the couch that pulled out. It was way better than having to sleep in a tiny room crammed with two beds and a bathroom. My favorite hotel is the one that had the indoor pool with the water slide. I can't remember where it was, and I don't remember what the name of it was. It's been a long time since we stayed there. I wish they had one of those hotels here. Wherever "here" is.

"Where are we?" I ask. My voice is hoarse from not having used it in so long.

My mom looks back at me through the rearview mirror. "Nashville."

I don't know anything about Nashville. I don't have time to compare what I see of Nashville to North Carolina because Dad comes back. "We're on the second floor." We park and Mom helps Dad get the suitcases. We walk together into the hotel and up the elevators to the room. Dad is tired from driving so long. Mom is too. This room does not have a separate bedroom. Mom and Dad lay down on one bed. I lay down on the other and grab the remote to the TV. It is only about six o clock in the morning, though, so nothing is on. I turn it off again and lay down. I stare at the heavy curtains on the window while my parents sleep. But I slept in the car, so I am not sleepy anymore. I get up and grab the tan colored ice bucket. I sneak out of the room and walk down the hallway towards the ice machine. A couple of girls, around my age, are sitting on the floor outside one of the rooms. They are looking at a cell phone and laughing. I jerk my eyes away. But I have to pass them to get to the ice machine. They are still laughing. I can't help but notice that their pajamas look new. And the tops match the bottoms. I've just got an orange t shirt and a pair of blue striped pajama pants on. It is comfortable but not pretty. I wish I hadn't left the room. The girls don't look up at me, though; they just keep whispering and laughing over whatever is on the cell phone. It probably belongs to one of them. I don't have my own cell phone. And I don't have a friend either. I wonder why they are in Nashville and start to make up reasons in my head.

Finally, I get to the ice machine. I used to think that the hotel ice machines were the coolest things in the whole wide world. I thought it was magic how I just had to push a button and perfectly shaped pieces of ice dropped out of the hole. I loved coming to the ice machine for the same reason I loved going to the vending machines. It was really neat watching how I could make something come out of one of the machines. I can't make anything happen in real life. On the way back to the room, I don't look at the girls. Instead, I look at the hotel's flower printed walls and dark carpets. I should get to know the place, I think to myself. We will be here for at least a few days, at least until Dad tricks someone into letting us rent a house. I get back to the room and close the door. My parents are still asleep. I sit down at the round, small table that's in the room. I pick up the hotel's pen and move the little pad of paper with their logo closer to me. I write the word "Nashville" three times, each in a different size and way than the first. Then I write the word "home" under it. I look at it for a minute, but then take the pen again. This time, I scratch the word "home" out. I don't have one of those.

A good part of living in a hotel is the breakfast. Almost all hotels offer continental breakfasts. Cold stuff like cereal and bagels. The good hotels offer better stuff, too, like oatmeal and toast. Orange juice or milk. The breakfasts start really early and only last a couple hours, so you have to be quick. No sleeping in. But it's worth it. Most hotels have an area set up with tables and microwaves and dispensers for the milk and juice. At least one television is usually in the breakfast area, turned to the local news station. Going down there almost makes you feel like you have a real kitchen. Another good part is how, right when you walk into the lobby, there's usually a shelf or two holding flyers and pamphlets that show off that city's attractions. There are usually dozens of these in each hotel. When you're really bored or riding the elevators up and down, or of going to the ice machine, looking at the pamphlets and making pretend itineraries is a good way to pass the time. I pretend I'm just a visitor, passing through, and looking for something fun to. Sometimes I even sort the fliers and pamphlets into piles of what I'd most like to do. So those things are cool. Having a vending machine full of candy at all times in the same building that you're living is also pretty neat. It's also neat never having to make your own bed or clean your room. Because maids do that for you every day of the week. You get fresh towels and soap every morning. Your trash is taken out. Even the carpets are vacuumed, and you don't have to lift a finger. So that's pretty neat. But the best part of living in a hotel is always having a pool you can hang out at. When choosing which hotel to stay at, a pool isn't only nice, it's a necessity. If a hotel does not have an indoor pool, we won't stay there. That might seem crazy to you but, believe me, it's not.

If there was no pool, you would pretty much be stuck inside a room with nothing but two beds and a TV twenty four hours a day. With your parents sitting right beside you. All the normal teenage stuff that I'm supposed to be doing…. I can't do. I can't listen to music because it's too loud. I can't talk on the phone because I don't have any friends to call and, even if I did, I still couldn't call them because it would be long distance and the phones in most hotels won't allow you to make long distance calls without putting a deposit down at the front desk first. A deposit is cash. So… no talking on the phone. When your parents want to go to bed, you have to go to bed, because they can't turn out the lights if you're still reading or watching television. There's only one bathroom which means you have to take turns taking showers and peeing. Basically, there is no such thing as privacy when you live in a hotel with someone else.

Unless there's a pool.

I get out of the room by going to the pool. I swim, I read books. And you meet people too. It's like looking into a picture book of what life is supposed to be like. Families on vacation. School trips. Couples on their honeymoon. People from other countries. Believe me, you meet all sorts of people at the pool in hotel rooms. Especially the hot tub. The hot tub is like the mall. People talk in the hot tub. And then sometimes, like after check-out but before check-in, there's nobody in the pool area except you. That's the best time to be there because, for just a little while, you don't have a mask to wear. You don't have to think about anything. You don't have to worry about the sleeve of your t-shirt that you wear into the water floating up and somebody seeing a scar. You don't have to worry about what to say. You don't have to hear someone ask you, "so where're you from" for the dozenth time. None of that. You just *are*. And, for a little while, you don't have to share---not your space, not your food, not your time, not anything.

I hate moving.

One day, when I turn eighteen, I'm going to pick a house and I don't care if I have to eat beanie weenies for the rest of my life in order to do it, I will never move. Never, not ever. Mom used to tell me to pretend I was on an adventure. As we packed up the car, she'd ask me what country we were going to. I usually said, "the mountains" because I thought the mountains were so far away they must be a different country. Mom never corrected me. We were in the mountains then, and she'd ask me what we saw. Sometimes we saw flowers as we pulled ourselves by the sheer strength of our arms up the side of the mountain. Mountain climbing is treacherous stuff---one wrong move, and you can fall to your death. Most of my adventures take place at the place, though. They always have. My favorite is to imagine that I'm a swimmer training for the Olympics. That's what I'm pretending now. I push my arms, one after the other, all the way through the water, over my head, again and again. My hair is tied back into a bun. I swim from one end of the pool to the other and then do it again, without stopping. After touching the edge the third time, I have to stop. I'm out of breath and very tired. I put my arms on the edge of the pool and lay my head in them, trying to catch my breath.

"Wow, you're a great swimmer."

I hadn't heard anyone come into the pool area so I'm surprised. I look up to see a grown man sitting in the hot tub watching me. He's got blonde hair and a big smile. I had no idea he'd been watching me. I shrug a little, mumble "thanks." I pull myself out of the water and walk over to the hot tub. Usually, I wouldn't get in the hot tub if only one person is in it. But there's something about the guy's voice that makes me feel it's okay. And sometimes, when you never get to talk to anybody, you'll do things you don't usually do for the chance to talk.

"My name's Jack." He said.

"Taya."

The water is so hot I can't get all the way in yet. I put my legs in and splash the water up on my legs, trying to get used to the heat.

"Do you take lessons?" Jack asks. He's got a hairy chest. Dad doesn't. He's barely got any chest hair.

"Lessons?"

"Swim lessons."

"Oh. No. I—I've never taken lessons. I just swim a lot."

He nods. "I used to be on a swim team. But that was ages ago."

I don't know what to say to that so I don't respond. I know what he's going to ask next. I wish he wouldn't. But I know he will because we are, after all, in a hotel and it's what everybody asks.

"Where you from?"

I hate this question.

What it's really asking is "Where did you grow up?" "Which city has a little bit of your DNA carved into it somewhere?" "Where have you lived most of your life?" "Where are you from" is a question that asks where someone's roots were planted. The answer is supposed to be easy; it's not supposed to require much thought. I mean, everybody knows where home is.

Unless you're me.

If you're me, you've spent most of your childhood in the backseat of a car, usually on the interstate. The hum of a car engine and eighteen wheelers are lullabies. If you're me, you've had far too many homes to count or to remember. Nothing is permanent, the knowledge that all is temporary is engrained into your soul so much that when you're awakened in the middle of the night to start riding to some new, unknown destination.... THAT feels normal. The grounds in over half the states have already known my footprints. Too many cities to count... or to even remember. The question, "where are you from?" always stumps me. How am I supposed to answer? Do I tell them the name of the last city I lived in for a month? Or maybe the name of the last state I called "home" is better, for some reason? Maybe just say the name of whatever place I currently like the best... or the first that comes to mind? Memphis.... I could always say Memphis because that's where I was born.... although my personal knowledge of Memphis is limited to a couple months' stay when I was in the third grade.

I give my usual answer.

"Well, my dad's part of the army, so we move around a lot."

This is part lie, part truth.

Dad *used* to be in the army. When he was, like, eighteen. He got a dishonorable discharge for desertion. Naturally. But when you tell people that your family is in the army, they never think it's weird that you're always moving. When I was younger, my answer to this question was different. I'd say, "My dad's job keeps us moving." But that caused too many questions. They wanted to know what he did for a living. What was I supposed to say? *Stealing?* I'd rather be an army brat than a convict's daughter. I mean, after all, whatever kind of person your parents are is the kind of person strangers think you are.

The guy nods as if he completely understands. "That must be rough, moving all the time."

You have no idea, I want to answer. But I don't. Instead, I just shrug.

"Well, we're just passing through. We're from Ohio but my wife, she wanted to go to the Opry show tomorrow night that's at Ryman. Have you ever been to the Ryman?"

I shake my head. I've never even heard of the Ryman. He tells me a little bit about his wife and the show they want to see. He says the Opry shows are on the radio, and have been for years and years. He grew up listening to them. His mama had cancer but, every week, she would just smile so big when it was time to listen to the show on the radio. They'd play cards, Rummy, and listen to Porter Wagoner and others from the static-filled speakers of the radio. When his mom died finally from the cancer, his dad hadn't been able to listen to the show anymore. And tomorrow night would be the first time he'd heard it in ten years. It would be the first time he'd seen it in person too. He probably wouldn't have brought tickets on his own, you know, to something he could listen to on the radio. But his wife wanted to come see it. It was really for her.

It's amazing what people will tell strangers about their personal lives. You can learn somebody's whole life history by sitting in the hot tub of a hotel.

I get tired of the hot tub before he does. Or maybe it's not the hot tub I tire of. Maybe it's not being alone anymore. It's hard work being polite. I gather up my towel and water bottle and tell him goodbye. I tell him to enjoy the show tomorrow night.

"Oh hey, thanks," he says. "Hope you like your new house."

Right, I think in my head, *The one you think we're just waiting to be ready for.* Actually, I don't even care what the house looks like anymore. I will like any house we find as long as I can have my own bedroom.

***** ***** *****

It's been almost a month of living in the hotel room when Dad comes in one day and holds out the key to a house. We've been tricking the people at the hotel for a week now. Dad's told them he's an executive for a computer company here on business; the business is going to pay for our stay at checkout. He gave them a fake credit card number to hold but they only run the card at checkout. The problem is that we're never going to officially "checkout." We're just going to leave.

I don't think about any of that.

I don't really understand how it all works. All I know for sure is that we get breakfast every morning and McDonalds is right across the street for lunch and dinner. Dad has money somehow and we've got a bed to sleep on. Even though it's not true, I tell myself that that's what matters.

Even though I'm ready to leave the hotel, in a way, it makes me sad too. I mean, Dad almost never messes with me in the hotel rooms, because Mom's always right there. Every once in awhile, she'll go to the store and Dad will secretly hide her room key so that, when she gets back, she'll be locked out until one of us opens the door. He does that to make sure she doesn't walk in and see what he does to me. But, like I said, it don't happen much at the hotel. So, in a way, it's kind of sad to be leaving. At least I'm safe here. But... as terrible as it is to admit it, I'm almost happier to leave the hotel. I need my own space so much. I can't share the same little room anymore. And I don't even care about the breakfast anymore. I don't even go down there every morning like I used to.

As we ride in the car away from the hotel, it really does feel like we're on an adventure. The car vibrates beneath me. The air from the vents blow on my face. We cross a bridge and the skyscrapers are behind us now. We drive for a long time. Then we turn off the freeway. There are trees now on either side of the road, and houses. I don't know why, I don't know what makes me feel like it, there's just this feeling that comes over me the more I see of

Nashville. I like it. I can tell it will be a very important part of my life.

The new house is pretty.

It's big. It's got two stories, with siding and a working fireplace. Mom tells me to pick my room and I walk through the house, looking at each bedroom. I don't really care about size of the room. I just need to make sure that whatever bedroom I pick has its own bathroom. I choose the master bedroom and go to help Mom and Dad unpack the car.

For now at least, the adventure is over.

We've been here a couple months already but it still doesn't really feel like home. The first thing we do when we move to a new place is paint the bedroom walls. Mom and I go shopping and I get to pick out a gallon of whatever color I want. I always choose some shade of blue. This time, I chose a cobalt blue that's got a shine to it. We go back to the house, change into old clothes, turn music up and paint.

After that, Mom spends a day or two hanging pictures up on the walls. Most of them are of me throughout the years, but there are a few of her and Dad. There are a few of still life that she's brought at yard sales or Target too. All of this is supposed to help make the new house feel like a home. In a way, it kind of works. I mean, it is neat seeing a white, bare wall turn into something colorful. And it's even neater having a space all my own. Nobody comes in my room without knocking on a door first. And it doesn't matter if I'm not tired when

Mom and Dad go to bed because we're not in the same room anymore---I can still read or watch television or play on the computer. When we first move into a new house, that's when I realize again that living in a hotel isn't really an exciting adventure. It's hard.

I started this new school.

Starting a new school in the middle of the year is not an easy thing to do. By the time you start, everybody else already has friends. You're pretty much just out of luck unless you're super pretty or an athlete.

I'm neither of those things.

But, so far, it's okay. Nobody makes fun of me too much. They just kind of ignore me. The hardest part of the day is lunch. I sit at whatever table I can find that's empty. I like to people-watch. I watch what they're wearing. I pretend I can hear what they're saying and I decide, based on how they behave at lunch, whether or not I could ever be friends with them. Most of the time, the answer is *no*.

Today, I'm trying to focus in on the girls. I know a lot of their names. I know the ones that are cheerleaders and the ones that are nerds. I know the ones that are quiet and the ones that are obnoxious. I see the ones all dressed in black and then there's Rachelle, who showed up Monday to school completely bald. She said she thought it was cool. I think it's kind of funny. The popular ones, they're the ones that are loud all the time, either laughing or cutting up. But it's the ones like me, the quiet ones, who know the most about everyone. The popular cheerleader can't tell you that Amy tried a cigarette for the first time on the smoking porch yesterday because the popular cheerleader only cares about the three or four girls who are always around her. I know that Lindsay doesn't have any money because I've watched her choose a hot pocket from the lunch line, then have to put it back when she didn't have enough coins to cover it three times this week. Three times, she's gone hungry at lunch. I know because I don't have friends so that means I have time to watch Lindsay in the food line. Usually, I wonder about the girls I see in the cafeteria, what they're going to do after school.

But not today.

I have a problem today.

The school has an annual Father Daughter Dance. It's Friday night. *This* Friday night. All the girls are excited about it. I've heard some talk about how their moms are taking them to buy a new dress for the dance. They are happy that their dads are going to come all dressed up and dance with them.

Kelsey, her dad's not coming. But that's because she doesn't have a dad anymore. She only lives with her mom and hasn't seen her dad since she was a baby. She keeps saying it's not a big deal. I wish I could think that way too.

But the truth is, it *is* a big deal. The school says there will be food, door prizes and a whole bunch of other stuff. Most importantly, the fathers will be there. They will be there to dance with their daughters.

I picture it in my head.

Me, dancing around the room in a beautiful dress. My hair in curls or maybe in a high bun with glitter sprinkled in it. Music is playing and a tall man is spinning me around the dance floor. Everyone sees him. He is tall and has a great big smile on his face. He laughs when I say something funny and he bends his head to listen quietly when I speak. We look alike. I have his long nose and his high cheekbones. When we're not dancing, he tells the other girls about something wonderful I've done. I have a dad just like they do, one who thinks that coming to a Father Daughter Dance is fun and special. I have a dad too, a dad who loves me.

That's what I picture in my head.

That's what I want, and I want it very much.

But.

My problem is that I can't even ask my dad. How am I supposed to go if I can't even ask him to come? My problem is that just the thought of asking him to come to a dance with me… it just gives me the creeps a little. My problem is that, if I stop to think about it, I don't know if I could handle dancing with him on a dance floor anywhere. It's like I have to decide just how badly I want to show my classmates that I'm just like they are. How badly do I want what they have, that's the question.

I haven't been able to think about anything else all day. I watch the girls at school. I think about how their dads already know about the dance, and about how easy it was for the girls to ask them to come. I think about how their dads would never have even thought of saying no. I stare at my tray of food; use my fork to push around some carrots. White. I'd want a white dress. It would be satin and simple. No sequins or anything. Just white satin and maybe it would have a bow around the waist. Mom has a pearl necklace and bracelet set I know she'd let me borrow. A night to be beautiful. A night to be a princess. A night to really be … whole.

I shake my head, pick up my tray and walk to the trash can. I toss the food and then head to my locker. As I do, my fingers grab my opposite wrist and gently rub over the scars.

I'm not whole.

But maybe…. Just maybe, I could be.

****** ***** *****

It's Tuesday now. Another day has passed. The dance is only three days away. He passed my test.... Last night was the end of the secret test. I told myself that if he came to my room before today, I wouldn't ask him. But he didn't. It's been a whole seven days since he came to my room. That's a very long time. Usually, he doesn't stay away for more than four nights in a row. *Something* usually happens before a full week has passed. Once, I thought he was going to make it a full week but then, on the fifth day, I was standing at the kitchen counter, eating an apple, and he walked behind me and grabbed my butt. *Something* always happens.

So I dared him. He didn't know about the dare but it was still there. I dared him to stay away from me, and to keep his hands to himself, for a full week. If he passed my dare, I'd ask him to take me to the Father Daughter Dance. But if he screwed it up, then it would be like proof that I couldn't depend on him. And I wouldn't ask him.

He passed the dare.

A full week with nothing.

I sat through dinner and tried about five times to bring it up. Every time I started to, though, my mouth filled with cotton and I said nothing.

What if he said no?

What if he didn't want to take me?

What if he laughed?

Sitting on my bed, I flip open Teen Magazine. Pictures of beautiful dresses pop back at me. It's almost as though they know it's time for the Father Daughter Dance. Midway through the magazine, I see it. I pick the whole thing up and pull it closer to my face. A white, satin gown. It has a gold bow around the waist. And the teen wearing it even has the same dirty blonde hair color I do. It could be me in that dress.

I don't think about it another second. I drop the magazine and run out of the bedroom. I race down the stairs and find Dad in the living room. He's watching the news and Mom is sitting in her recliner sewing. They both look up when I come in the room.

"Hey," Mom says.

"Hi." I sit down on the edge of the couch and swallow past the lump in my throat. That's what I have to do to find the courage. I open my mouth to speak but can't ask him. All I see in my head is his face in my mind, his eyes squeezed shut, his mouth taut. I give up, slump back against the couch, lowering my chin to touch my neck. So stupid, thinking I could ever ask him to go. And what kind of person *am* I anyway, to even want to ask him?

We listen to the weather report before Mom says, "So, Taya, how's school going?"

I shrug.

"Do you have anything due this week?" Mom asks.

I shake my head. And then, without even intending to, I add, "There's a dance Friday."

"A dance?" Mom asks.

I nod.

"What kind of dance?" Dad asks, frowning, looking toward me for the first time since I sat down.

I stare at my legs. I could brush it off. Say it was some sort of dance for the kids. That's what I should do. I know it is. But, I don't know why, I say, "It's a… you know… Father Daughter thing."

For a second, no one speaks. Then Dad says, "A Father Daughter dance? At your school?"

"Hm, yeah, it's, you know, something I guess they do every year."

"Well, you two oughta go to that." Mom perks in.

Dad doesn't say anything for a long time. So long in fact that my face starts to turn red. Of course he doesn't want to go. Why would he?

"Do you want to go to it?" Dad asks me. He doesn't sound mad. He sounds… interested. I brave a glance, a quick one, at his face. Whatever I see makes me shrug one shoulder instead of scoffing.

"Of course she does," Mom says.

Dad smiles. "It would be really fun. I haven't been to a dance in ages."

"So you'd go?" I ask.

"Oh, of course. It'll be fun. What time is it on Friday?"

"Eight."

He turns the television off and winks at me. "Be ready in your best then at seven thirty."

I don't want to admit it or nothing but... but as I watch him walk away, a little tiny piece of me is... hopeful.

****** ****** ******

It's funny how clothes can make you feel like a different person. Mom took me shopping too. Just like the other girls' moms at school. I told her I wanted a white satin dress and, after going to four different places, we finally found one. I showed Mom the picture in the magazine of the white dress with the gold bow and she found some gold satin material and made a bow for me. It's perfect. It's beautiful. It goes to the floor and even came with a white satin arm wrap that helps cover my scars. As long as I'm careful with that, no one will see them. And when I look in the mirror, I think for a few minutes that maybe I am pretty. I love how the silk feels so soft against my skin and how the glitter in my hair makes me sparkle. Looking in the mirror, you'd never think I'm anything but a normal teenager. A special one.

Dad is waiting for me in the living room when I come downstairs. He's got on a dark blue tuxedo. He looks real good. And he's smiling. He never smiles when he looks at me. Maybe tonight will be more than just a dance. Maybe it will be a night to start over, all over, fresh. Maybe it will remind him that I'm just his daughter.

All I can think about in the car is how pretty the sky is. There are tons of stars out. It makes me want to wish on one except that, right now, I don't know what I'd wish for. I'm still a little scared. Dad is very unpredictable. Sometimes he's really kind. Sometimes he's not. But I'm more than scared. Mostly, in fact, I'm excited. I can't wait for the other kids to see me and my dad together. I can't wait to twirl around and feel the earth spinning like in a fairytale. Except this fairytale is more important than if I were dancing with a prince. This fairytale is real.

The dance is in the school gym. There are all kinds of decorations. The theme is "I Will Remember You" and it's written in a large banner across one wall. There's table where all the girls and Dads are getting name tags. I guess so that the dads can know each other's names. Several girls are already dancing with their dads.

Dad puts his hand on my back to guide me over to the punch table. That's when I first start to feel a little weird. I don't like his hand on my back. But I'm too excited to be here to really care.

"Do you see any of your friends?" Dad asks. *No*, I think in my head, *I don't have friends. You're my dad. Shouldn't you know that?* But instead of saying that, I just shake my head.

I stare at the dance floor. I see the people moving. Dancing is what I had dreamed of. But I'm not about to ask Dad to dance. I know better. A girl comes up and I'm in the way. She's trying to get to the punch behind me. I move to the side, away from the table. Dad smiles at her and then takes my hand. "We're here to dance, right?" He asks. We walk onto the floor and he pulls me close. My whole body goes rigid. It is a slow song and all the dads are holding their daughters close like this, though, so I don't say anything.

"Do you like my tuxedo?" Dad asks, putting his chin on my head.

I don't answer him.

"I picked blue because I know it's your favorite color."

That's when I know. Coming was a bad idea.

I don't feel beautiful anymore. I just feel weird. But I pretend I don't. I try to smile and say, "It's nice." The music is slow so I can watch the other girls dancing with their dads. They all seem to be having fun. Some are laughing. The dads are smiling. They are talking to each other. I'm the only one wondering how much longer this song can last. It's too hard to pretend when his hand is rubbing circles on my back. It's too hard to pretend when I have to work so hard to keep the memory of ten nights ago out of my head. I feel nothing like these other girls. I am the alien I thought I was. Maybe make-up can cover up the scars on my arms... but it can't cover up my insides.

The air suddenly has more oxygen in it when the song is over and I get away. I tell Dad I have to go to the bathroom. I stand in front of the mirror and force myself to take really deep breaths in and then breathe out. Two girls walk in laughing. I stand up quickly and walk out before they realize someone stupid is in their way.

****** ***** ******

I last for three songs. I dance three dances before I've had all I can take. I tell Dad I'm tired, that we can go home. So we do. We drive home and the whole time, Dad talks about how fun it was. I stare out the window.

I go straight to my room when we get home. Mom is in the shower. I hear when she gets out. Then I hear the bedroom door shut down the hall. And I lie on the bed and wait. I'm not dumb. I know what's going to happen. Ten days is the longest I'll ever get. It's after one in the morning before my bedroom door opens.

As he pulls the edge of my gown up to my chin, Dad says, "Do you know how long I'd waited for you to dance with me like that?" I feel my stomach churning but it's the taste of the salty tears rolling into my mouth that breaks my heart. It doesn't even hurt tonight. I can't even feel it. I don't even try to stop him. How can I? I'm the one who asked him to go to the dance. I'm the one who started this. Maybe if I wasn't so stupid, I could have had two weeks without feeling the ants inside my veins. Maybe if I wasn't so stupid, I could have had forever. All I wanted was a dream. What I got was another nightmare.

I am really, really sore. My eyes are bloodshot and tired. Mom and Dad have been fighting all day long every day for the past three days. Dad thinks the cops are catching up to us again. Mom doesn't want to leave until we're sure. She says we don't have the money to go anywhere right now. She wants to wait, she thinks he's paranoid. I skipped school today because I can't concentrate on anything. My head hurts. I feel stupid for crying just because they're fighting. Except it's not just because they're fighting that I'm crying. When they fight, Dad makes himself feel better by coming to me. Last night, he was in my room forever and he was mad, still, so it was really bad. He held my head to him. I started to gag and he got even angrier. I didn't mean to gag, I just couldn't help it. It's like someone's pouring boiling water into my heart and it's almost full and if it gets too full, it'll just burst open. The heart can break, you know. It can and I think mine is really close to breaking.

I've been cutting more. It helps but it doesn't take the memories away. This morning,

I woke up and screamed because when I opened my eyes, I saw Dad's face over mine. Only he wasn't really there anymore. And then I hear them yelling at each other and throwing things all day and it just makes me want to scream. But I can't, I can't scream, because that will just make it worse.

I take my nails and scratch at my arms. I scratch them hard and I don't stop. I'm trying to get the ants that are inside out. They make my skin crawl and it's hard to think. They make me feel crazy. Something crashes so hard into the wall that it makes framed pictures fall from the wall. I know that's what happened because I know the sound of frames hitting the floor really well. I hear glass shatter.

I stop scratching my arms and roll into a fetal position on my bed. I take the pillow and pull it down over my ears. I pull the edges hard, trying to block all the sounds. I need to get out of the house but I can't, because to get out, I'd have to walk right past them. I look around the room and see the window. I'm on the second story but I wonder…

I go to it and open it up. I claw at the screen until I rip a hole in it and then I make it bigger. Big enough for me to stick my head through. I look around. I couldn't jump… but there's a ledge. I might be able to walk along the ledge until I could jump to the lower roof. From there, I could… No. They'd hear me jumping on the roof and come to see. Mom would have a heart attack and Dad would just get mad.

I'm trapped.

That's what it feels like. Trapped by violence.

*****   ******   *******

We are learning about the slaves in school. We learned that some of them fought for freedom. Some of them risked their entire lives, and the lives of their families, to be a part of the Underground Railroad. Not only slaves but free white men and women took part in the Underground Railroad. Their whole purpose was to get the slaves to freedom, to get them to safety. We have to watch this video in class on it and that's what they said on the video…. That they risked everything to get to safety. I stare down at my notebook and write the word, "Safe" four times in the margins.

What is safety?

I don't know what that word is. It is foreign. It's like it's part of another language. I don't know what it means. I whisper it while I'm sitting in the chair at school. "Safe." "Safe." I think of the fighting that's been going

on for days inside my house. Calm. If
something is safe, it is calm. I think of Dad,
grunting and thrusting again and again inside of
me, hard, until I think I'm going to rip into a
thousand pieces. Safety is space. No fuss. No
complaint. Never, ever disagree lest it explode
into a physical struggle. Please the adults in my
life without question. If Dad says jump, I'm
going to jump. If he says "roll over", I'm going
to roll over. Why? Because, if I don't, I might
be struck. Because, if I don't, he won't leave.
Because, if I don't, safety will continue to be a
dream. I can't get mad because anger steals
peace. The reward for being the poster child for
obedience is a reprieve that comes every
morning. They might fight and crash through
walls all night long but, by morning, they will
tire and stop. Dad might stay in my room for
hours. He might grab my breasts so tight it
hurts. I might have to do things I don't want to
do. But if I just breathe and obey, he will go
away.

But that's not really safety.

It's more like temporary safety.

The slaves, they fought and died and
risked death just for the *chance* to be safe
forever. They were brave, those slaves. Nobody
would shoot me if I told what he does to me.
They might not believe me. They might not
care. They might not even stop it. But they
wouldn't kill me over it. Dad would get mad, he

might hit me. But not even he would really hurt me for it. I'm just not as brave as the slaves, I am too afraid of the unknown.

So I just lay still. I feel my insides get all jumbled up, I can feel my heart hurting. But I just lay still. It's not brave. It's not strong. It's not safe. It's scared. And that's what I am, scared.

****** ***** *****

I didn't know it was normal to bleed the first time. When I was nine years old and he did it, I didn't know it was normal to see so much blood. I just knew I was bleeding. He bought me a washcloth, tried to help me clean myself up, but I didn't want him to touch me. I kept scooting away from his hand, bending my knees up, trying to get him to stop. He got mad at me, grabbed my bloodied panties and sheets and walked out of the room. He didn't tell me it was normal.

I thought I was dying.

I was afraid of going to sleep. I thought if I went to sleep, I would bleed to death. So I stayed awake. I was afraid to lay down because I was afraid that if I laid down, I'd go to sleep, so I sat up the whole time. I remember pulling down my panties and bending way over to look at my bottom, trying to figure out if it was still bleeding. I was scared to go to the bathroom because I thought more blood would come out, not pee. I'd felt it rip, I felt it tear. I knew something was broken now, I knew something was gone. But I didn't know it happened to everybody. So I freaked out a little. I started walking real, real slow so that I wouldn't start bleeding again. I wore two pairs of panties so that anymore blood wouldn't get on my clothes.

It took a long time for me to stop worrying I was dying. A couple months anyway. I don't know what I would have done a few years later when I started my period if I hadn't read enough books by then to know that it had been normal. Everybody bled. At least all girls do.

When you're afraid of something, though, it takes over your life. Like now. Now, I'm not as afraid of Dad as I am of their fights. I know Dad isn't going to hurt me physically. Not like he does Mom. She hurts him too but he's stronger. I know he's stronger. And if he gets too mad, it would be real easy for him to hurt her. That's what I'm most afraid of. It seems like the fights are getting even worse.

Dad says he's leaving.

Mom doesn't want him too.

Dad wants us all to get packed and into the car right now. He thinks the cops are close. He doesn't want to go back to jail. Mom isn't moving. She says she's done. She doesn't want to drive across the country anymore. She tells him he needs to grow up. This morning, when I went down for school, I saw Mom in the kitchen and she had a cut on her forehead. Her arm was hurt too: she was holding it funny.

I am sitting with my headphones on, loud music blaring into my ears, but I don't hear a single word they're singing. All I can think about is everything that's being broken downstairs. Broken glass, broken frames, broken homes.

I don't know what makes me do what I do next. I don't know what even makes me think it. All I know is that one minute I'm sitting on the bed and the next minute, I'm pulling my cell phone out of my backpack.

"Police, Fire and Rescue, how may I help you?"

I swallow.

"Hello? Police, Fire and Rescue, can I help you?"

"I---" Courage almost makes me hang up. But I think of the slaves. They dragged their little children into the Underground Railroad. Some of them *sent* their children by themselves. All because they were searching for *lasting* safety. "I—I think I can help you find somebody you've been looking for." And then I say Dad's name and our address. Then I hang up.

***** ****** ******

I expect guns and sirens and everything you see on TV. But nothing happened. Not even a knock on the door. Nothing. The fight keeps going on until I fall into a restless, exhausted sleep. I wake up to silence. I get dressed and go downstairs, expecting to find Dad gone and Mom crying.

Dad is in the kitchen pouring coffee into a mug. I don't know where Mom is but I bet she's still asleep. My heart is racing. Now I'm scared that maybe he knows what I did. Maybe he knows I called the cops. But he just says, "good morning" and walks out of the kitchen.

I grab a blueberry muffin and my backpack; tell him I'm going to walk to school today. Mom usually takes me but I know she can't today. Maybe it's a good thing that the cops didn't care. I don't think Mom could handle anything else right now.

All day at school, it's there in the back of my mind. I think about it in my head. I picture him being arrested while I'm at school. I can't wait to get home and see what's happened. Mom will tell me. I wonder if they will tell him who called. Do they know who called? I didn't tell them who I was. I didn't tell them anything except his name and address. They're the cops after all. They should be able to find out who he is. That he's wanted in about four different states.

When I get home, though, he's in the living room, working on a computer. My heart falls into my feet. And I thought I was stupid. The police here must be even more stupid than me. I mean, I *gave* them an address. What else could they possibly need?

Mom seems tired still but she cooks dinner. She offers to help me with my homework. But I tell her I got it, then I go upstairs and she goes to their bedroom too. It is after ten when I hear the strong knock on the door.

My heart starts beating like mad thing. I know Dad's downstairs in the living room because I can hear the television. I walk to my bedroom door and open it. But I don't go downstairs; I just stand at the door. Dad pulls open the door and then jerks. For a split second, I think he's going to run.

But he knows better.

Mom must have heard the cops' voices because she comes out of the bedroom and walks past me downstairs. She is crying. Dad is calm. The cops are putting handcuffs on him. It's all so calm and peaceful like. I don't move. I just stand there, watching from the top of the staircase. Mom and Dad kiss and then Dad looks up. He catches my eye. I swallow past the chill in my bones. I'm not happy. I'm not sad. I'm not angry.

But I am safe.

I had this jewelry box one time. It was made of glass. Pretty dumb, giving a six year old something made out of glass. When you opened it up, there was a beautiful ballerina in a pink tutu that twirled around and around to a melody. I loved that jewelry box. I loved it so much that I never put anything inside it, because I was afraid that it would make it dirty. It wasn't long after Dad gave it to me that we moved again. Instead of taking it with us, I put it in a small box all by itself to pack. I thought it would be safer that way. We left Virginia for good that time, and moved to South Carolina instead. I couldn't wait to get our stuff and unpack my ballerina box. I couldn't wait to see the pretty glass, and the ballerina twirl and twirl.

We got a small apartment and every day after school I would race inside from the bus excitedly asking if the stuff had come yet. Finally, it got there. We started unpacking everything one by one. I looked everywhere for the small box. Mom found it first and gave it to me. I took it all by itself into my room and shut the door. I didn't want anything to interrupt me as I opened it up. It was like getting the prettiest thing I had ever had all over again. It was like being given the bestest gift all over again. My stomach was flip-flopping, I was so nervous and excited and happy. Happy. I was happy. Really and truly happy. I wasn't scared. I wasn't lonely. I wasn't tired. I wasn't numbed. I was happy. But when I opened the box up and took the jewelry box out, all my stupid happiness turned to shock. I hadn't put any newspaper in the box with it and the movers didn't know what was in the box. They didn't know it was glass, they didn't know that it was glass. They weren't careful with it. And right across the entire top of the box was a long crack in the glass. It still opened. The ballerina still twirled. But the crack on the outside of the box made the whole thing ugly.

I cried. I cried and cried and cried. I cried until I didn't think I had any more tears in me. I stared into the glass on top of the box. The crack distorted my face. Dad thought I was being stupid because it still worked. Mom said she would try to get me another one. But I didn't want another one. I wanted the one I had loved so much. After I got done crying and being sad, I got mad. I was mad for a long time. If we hadn't had to move—again—then I wouldn't have had to put it in the box in the first place. If Mom had told me to put newspaper in the box around it, it might not have gotten broken. If the stupid movers had been more careful with our boxes, it might not have been broken. If Dad hadn't given it to me in the first place, I wouldn't have cared about something like a jewelry box. I was mad at everybody. Dad told me to stop being a baby about it. He told me I could still use it, that it still worked perfectly fine. He didn't get it. Nobody got it.

It was broke.

When something is broke, it is not the same anymore. When something is broken, it is damaged. When something is broke, it is ugly, even if it still works. When something is broke, it is useless. When something is broke, it cannot ever be seen the same way again. When something is broke, its value changes, it isn't worth as much anymore. When something is broke, it becomes nothing more than trash. I was only six years old then, I didn't know all of that.

All I did know was that I didn't want the jewelry box anymore. That very day, I walked it right to the kitchen and threw it in the garbage. Because that's what it was now that it was broken.

That was nine years ago.

I'm not six years old anymore, I'm fifteen. I'm in high school now. I should be happy about that. All the other kids seem like they are. But I'm not. It's not that I'm not happy about it, I just don't care. I don't have a boyfriend, but I don't care about that either. I get good grades, but I don't care about that either. We've been in this same house for a year now. That's like a record or something. That should make me really happy. And it's not that I'm not happy about that. I just don't care.

When something really good happens, I smile and laugh and act like I'm happy. But, really, it doesn't matter. Nothing really matters. I think about when I was six, before everything went to hell. I would open up the jewelry box and I would dance around the room. I would twirl, just like the ballerina twirled. I pretended I was the ballerina. I stood in front of the mirror in my room and put on dress up clothes. I thought I was just as good as the pretty ballerina in the pretty jewelry box. I was stupid. Now I pretend

I'm invisible. This is pretty easy to do, since nobody knows my name anyway.

Mom's calling my name. It makes me jump and pull the sleeve down over my wrist, so she can't see the crack. It must be time to go. We have to go see my dad. My stomach flip flops and panic bursts in my bones. But then I smother it. I grab my black, small purse from the floor and run out the bedroom door. Mom's ready to go, standing at the door. She's in a hurry. We have to be there before visiting hours are over or we won't get in. As it is right now, we'll only have an hour. I could drag my feet and kick and scream. I could go to the bathroom, pretend It has started and take forever. I could stall. It would make Mom furious. She probably wouldn't speak to me all night. Even if we go, when we get back, she's going to go into her bedroom and cry. That's what she does all the time. I could make it worse. But I don't. Because I don't care. We get in the car and the whole drive, that's what I tell myself: I don't care.

The knot in my stomach grows bigger when I see the barbed wire fence with the big circles at the top. It looks like a factory. But it's not. I know it's not. It looks civilized, maybe even like a small apartment complex might. But I know it's not. It's really chaos inside. The parking lot is dead silent. We walk into the building and there is noise. Three black women stand ahead of us, they are whispering. One is laughing. There is an older lady at the front of the line. She is standing with her head up, her arms clutched together in front of her. Mom rustles in her purse. There is two minutes to wait before it all can start. Behind the desk, there are four cops. One of them is a lady. She sits behind the desk. She is the one that will watch us write our names in the Visitor's Log. There are two male cops standing up. They have guns on. Their uniform has always made me nervous. There is another cop standing too. This one is a girl. I eye her. She is the one who will search me, because girls are not allowed to be searched by the boy cops. Only female cops can search girls. I eye her. She's got her dark hair pulled back into a bun. She is Mexican and her skin is smooth and tan-like. Her eyes are dark and narrowed.

Finally, the cop sitting tells the older lady to go ahead and write her name in the book. It has started. First, we write our names. Then we are searched. The female cop takes the older lady into a side room, and they come out a few minutes later. The older lady moves on to the next area of the room, where she will wait until everyone else gets through. It's funny. This is the part I dread the most, not when we actually see him.

It is my turn. I have to spread my arms and legs wide. The girl cop asks me my name, then takes a black wand-like thing and runs it over the top and underside of my arms, then my legs. I have to take off my shoes because I might have a knife in them. I even have to open my mouth so she can make sure nothing stupid is in there. She takes my purse, opens it and goes through the entire contents. I wonder what she thinks when she sees the Wrigley's pack of gum, the compact mirror and lipstick. I wonder what she thinks when she sees the tampon. Most of all, I wonder what she thinks when she sees the tiny stuffed rabbit I carry with me always. It looks like its a little kid's. But it's not. It's mine. I carry that rabbit everywhere; I found him in the woods in the back of our Indiana house. I thought it was such a cool thing to find. And rabbits' ears are supposed to be lucky, did you know that? If the rabbit's ear is lucky, I bet the whole rabbit is even luckier. Not that I believe in luck.

Everyone is through now.

The really tall male cop pushes a button next to the steel gray door and it opens. It is time to walk through. Mom has stopped talking now too. It is a long and hard thing, to get through the security. And we are always a little nervous. We walk into this huge room that looks like a cafeteria. There are tables everywhere and men in jumpsuits sitting at them. Some of them are standing, but they are all looking at us. Mom spots Dad first, and he waves.

Mom walks quickly ahead, I lag behind. They are hugging when I get there. Dad knows better than to hug me, so he just smiles and asks how I am instead. I lie and tell him I'm good. I get some change from my purse and say I'm going to get a Coke. I walk away, happy for the few minutes of freedom the Coke machine offers.

I don't even know why I have to come. When I get back to the table, all I do is sit and listen to them talk. I don't even know what it's all about. But it's the weirdest thing. I was all nervous and stuff being searched, and I didn't even want to come at all, but now... The numbed feeling is back. I don't care about anything he says. I see his mouth move, but I don't hear anything. I don't care about anything at all.

I don't want to admit it or anything but I know why. Nothing he says matters. Nothing he does matters. It doesn't matter that I have to spend an hour of my time here. The memories don't matter. Why? Because you can't hurt what's already broken.

My English teacher is weird. Really weird. I mean, when we talk about a book we just read for an assignment, she sits in a rocking chair like she's talking to first graders. And if you fall asleep in her class and she catches it, she pours half a glass of cold water over your head so you have to spend the rest of the day with wet hair and clothes. She's really weird.

The weirdest thing she's done so far is this assignment. We've been talking all week about tradition. How girls are usually not portrayed as the hero. We talked about what kind of trouble the people in fairytale usually face. Let me just tell you that most children's stories were not Disney. I mean, there were all kinds of bad things happening: kids getting ate, wolves scaring the pants off little girls, witches trying to kill off sixteen year old girls. Really, all the children's stories were quite violent.

We just finished talking about all the

traditional fairytales. Now we have to pick one and make it modern. Whatever problem the heroine faces in the traditional story, we have to make that a problem that kids really face today. We have to pick a social issue and make it work in one of the fairytales. Our new story has to have a realistic end to it too. No Prince Charming riding a white horse to save the day.

Weird.

But also kind of interesting. I keep thinking about it. I thought about it the rest of the afternoon in school. I thought about it on the way home and during dinner. I keep thinking about the fairytales that I've always heard.

I could use Little Red Riding Hood and make her get kidnapped. That happens all the time. Just yesterday, on the way to school, there was a new Amber Alert blinking over the freeway. I could have her kidnap and the kidnapper could be crazy. But... I don't know if Mrs. Simmons would think of kidnapping as a social concern or just a crime. And how would my Little Red Hiding Rood's end change? She'd have to be rescued. I could use Snow White... But what would the social concern be?

The next day in class, I still haven't thought of anything. We are given time to work on it in class. Not many of us are really working on it. Trey, behind me, is blowing bubble gum and acting like he's going to stick it in my hair. If he does, I'll kill him. A couple of the girls around me are writing out Prom Date choices. We're not Juniors or Seniors but it's still nice to pretend some upper classman will ask us to the dance. More are passing notes about Kelsey; half of us are pretty sure she's pregnant but we don't know if Greg or Zack is the baby's dad. She's missed, like, more than a week in a row and she told Olivia that she was late. Olivia told everybody else. If high school has taught me anything, it's taught me not to open my mouth unless what I'm going to say is ok for the whole school to know. Normally, I'd pass notes too but this time, I'm actually interested in the assignment.

I start going through the list of princesses again. But, one by one, I cross out the fairytales for one reason of another. I draw little hearts on my paper, then add arrows that are shooting through them. I doodle all the time. Even on the edges of my tests. When I stare at a math problem I don't know the answer to, I draw block F's on the edge of my paper. Then, sometimes, I draw stars and color them in with my pencil. I don't know why I draw the stars; maybe I'm just wishing it will help me know the answers.

Wishes.

It's like a light bulb goes off in my head. Cinderella! Cinderella wasn't kidnapped but she was forced to work like a slave by her stepmother. Her stepmother was jealous, that's why. Cinderella was old enough to get married—but she never disobeyed her stepmother. She only snuck out of the house once! Suddenly, my head is full of ideas. I jot them down, as fast as I can. Before I finish one sentence, I know something else about my story.

I never hear the bell ring. Only when Trey uses his notebook to slap me on the shoulder do I realize class is over. I shut my notebook and cram it into my backpack. "Writing the next big novel today, T?"

Trey is in almost every one of my classes. He's a nice guy…but he's also loud and obnoxious. When the teacher calls on him to answer a question, he almost always makes a stupid answer. Not because he doesn't know, but because he wants the kids to think he's funny. So I know better than to spoil my story by telling him anything. I shrug, walking out of the class.

But I can't wait to get home and finish the assignment.

***** ***** *****

It is past midnight. But I can't stop thinking about my assignment. I wrote three pages of it after dinner but then crumpled them up. See, in my story, Cinderella's parents died, leaving her with her cruel stepmother and stepsisters. At first, I made her rebellious… She snuck out all the time and refused to do the chores. But she probably wouldn't do any of that—not if her stepmother had abused her for years. The original version got that right… She probably would obey.

But she probably wouldn't be as happy as she was in the original version. I mean, she probably wouldn't feel like singing or any of that. She would have to be messed up. The question was how. I couldn't figure that part out and gave up trying. Now it's after midnight and the paper's due in two days. I turn my head to look out my window. The curtains are pulled back and I can see the black sky.

I'm still staring outside when my eyelids start to feel heavy. I fight it at first, roll to my other side; stare at the red numbers on the clock. But then I yawn real big and my eyes close.

I'm awakened when I feel someone sit on the edge of my bed. My eyes pop open. I know it is him. I don't move but my legs go stiff, my arms too. He lies down behind me, puts a hairy, heavy arm around my waist and pulls me back to him. "Come on, be good for your daddy," he whisper. He wants me to roll over. But I swallow back a scream instead and stay still. I feel his hands on me; I can feel the bile rolling in my stomach.

I don't know just when I stop feeling panicked. I don't know when I stop feeling at all. But when his breathing gets real heavy, I barely notice. When he pushes my head down, I do what he wants. I don't know why. When he grunts and hurts me real bad, I turn my head and squeeze my eyes shut. Tears leak from the corners, but I don't make a sound. I don't even breathe.

The first kiss from my daddy. I was nine years old. I was flipping channels on the TV and saw two people kissing. I said: "Eew" and turned it real fast. But he told me to go back. They weren't kissing anymore but Daddy asked me how I knew it was gross if I'd never tried it. He said he could prove it wasn't gross and leaned over. One minute, he was sitting beside me, the next minute, he had his tongue in my mouth. It was gross. And it freaked me out. I jumped up but he grabbed my hand, said if I told, he'd wear me out good. I didn't want to tell, I just wanted to erase it.

After that, I was never able to think of my daddy in the same way again. Cause of things like what happened tonight. But of all the things he does, kissing is the worst. It's worse, even, then when he sticks me. Kissing is special. Maybe that's why he always has to kiss me real hard before he leaves the room—because he wants it to be special. But it's not. It doesn't make me feel special at all.

I am shaking real bad when the door shuts. I still have my clothes on. I am glad I am wearing the old Winnie the Pooh T-shirt as a gown because if I had on pjs, he'd have had to take them off and I hate being naked. I am shaking so bad I have to grind my teeth to make it stop. I curl my legs up until they touch my chin and lay real, real still.

Maybe if I lay real still, I can feel normal. But instead, my stomach is in a big knot. I want to throw up but I don't. The noise in my head is so loud. It's like nails on a chalkboard. I squeeze my eyes shut, but then pop then open again. Closing them blocks the sound a little but it makes me see bad things. I lay there, feeling like I'm about to die, until I just can't take it anymore.

I jump up out of bed and over to my desk. It is white. White is a pretty color. That makes me cry again, because I am not pretty. I jerk open the middle drawer; throw out makeup and hair clips so I can reach into the very back. Finally, I find it.

A tiny wave of peace comes over my heart as I hold the pink razor in my hand. The tears stop flowing because I have to concentrate now. If I get it wrong, something really bad could happen. I think about it sometimes–doing the really bad thing. But I can't. I have to finish my English paper.

I turn my left palm over and, without even pausing, rake the edge of the razor sideways across my wrist. Blood spoons to the surface. I barely feel sting of the razor, but the sight of the blood makes me feel a little less panicked. It makes it hurt less. I let it bleed. The blood drips on the paper that's lying on my desk. I let it. It makes me feel better. Yes, I'm ugly, but it's because I have scars on my wrists and my arms.

It's ok. I can fix my wrist. I can fix this hurt. I can make it stop. I keep a washcloth in my room, under my bed. Finally, I pull it out and hold it against my wrist. Making it stop all by myself makes me feel a little better too–I do know how to do something good. It takes a few minutes for all the blood to go away. My wrist is red, scratched. Proof that I was hurt.

I look at all the scars on my wrists and arms. I grip my right hand with my left, and then use my left thumb to gently rub the scars that crisscross my right wrist. The scars are not bumpy, they are smooth. But I can feel where they start and where they end. I can tell how many times I have been hurt.

I stare out the window again. Only then do fresh tears dot my eyes. I blink, trying to keep them away, but then I give up and let them fall. I cry until my head hurts and my nose is stuffy. Then I just lay still and stare out the window. Just as my eyes start to get heavy again, Cinderella flashes in my mind and, suddenly, I know the rest of my story.

Once upon a time in a faraway land, there was a little girl. Her momma died giving birth. Her father remarried to a woman with two daughters of her own. He hoped that his little girl would become best friends with his new wife's daughters. He hadn't been married long when he died of a heart attack.

The little girl was very sad. She cried all day and all night. She remembered her daddy telling her stories and tucking her into bed. She remembered his hugs. She had never felt as cold as she did now. She needed to turn to her stepmother for comfort but the old woman didn't like the girl. She was prettier and kinder than her own two daughters. So instead of helping her, the stepmother told her that it was stupid that she had never been given any chores. Hard work, she said, would mend a broken heart.

So she gave the little girl a long list of chores. Her own daughters didn't have any chores. Soon, they started calling her Cinderella because she was always dirty from cleaning the floors and the clothes and the dishes.

The stepmother only allowed Cinderella to eat the family's leftovers and she was never allowed to eat from the same table as the other members of the family. Even though it was really her father's house, Cinderella grew up feeling like she was a servant.

She was alone all the time. There weren't any other servants to talk to because she did all the work. She couldn't talk to her stepsisters or stepmother. She was not allowed to go to school. She thought she should be grateful because she had a place to sleep, but she didn't feel grateful. She just felt sad.

She was so lonely that she started to talk to the animals. There was a horse and some mice that ran through the basement where she slept. She talked to them. She told them that she missed her father and that she could remember him because he had been the only person who had ever been kind to her. At first, she pretended the animals talked back to her but then she got older and thought that was stupid. So first, she stopped pretending they answered her. Then she quit talking to them at all.

One day, the stepsisters came home with new clothes. They were going to the special dance. They laughed at Cinderella because she only had one outfit and it was always dirty. She would never go to a dance. Cinderella watched them laugh and talk about their new things with the stepmother until she thought her heart was going to break. It was such a small thing, but it was so unfair. Who could she laugh with? Who was her friend?

Cinderella ran all the way to the basement, her room. She lay on the bed and cried. She wasn't loved. What would it feel like to have someone brush her hair the way she had seen Stepmother brush the stepsisters'? What would it feel like getting ready for a special dance, giggling and feeling excited? She would never know. The rock in her stomach got bigger. She sat up and, without thinking, reached over to the little nightstand and grabbed a glass that held some water. She should have already taken it back to the kitchen; it had sat here since the day before. Instead of taking it upstairs, though, Cinderella threw it across the room, as hard as she could. It smashed against the wall and shattered.

It made it just a little easier to breathe.

She should clean it. She didn't want Stepmother to come down and see it. She headed upstairs to get a broom but she stepped on a shard of glass. It cut her foot and she grabbed it, sitting in the floor. It had hurt.... But not really.

She stared at the tiny droplets of blood on the sole of her foot. Shouldn't a cut from glass hurt more than this? She looked beside her on the floor, grabbed another shard. She turned her hand over, examined it. Then she took the glass and used it to cut her hand. She didn't know why, but it made her feel better. Like it gave a reason for the pain. It didn't seem like so much to handle anymore.... It was just a little blood to clean.

Pretty soon, Cinderella cut her arms and legs and wrists a lot more. She wore long sleeves so nobody saw. It made the pain better---at first. But then, when the blood dried up, the pain came back. So she had to do it more.

When the stepsisters left for the school dance, Cinderella felt alone. She knew she wasn't wanted at the dance--but she was so tired of being hidden. She could see stars in the sky at night, and they were so bright. She had to try to see the stars closer.

She ransacked her closets and found a piece of blue cloth. It wasn't much but she knew she could sew it into a dress. With some ribbons and a bit of lace she'd grabbed from her stepsister's room, she soon had the blue cloth turned into a dress. It wasn't perfect, but it would do. She used her horse to ride off the property, and she asked directions from a neighbor tending the yard. She was happy. She was excited. She was going to shine for just a minute too. Maybe she could even dance. Out here, away from the basement, the stars were so much brighter and they seemed to twinkle at her.

No one knew who she was. They all said that they hadn't seen her at the school before. But they didn't laugh at her either. Cinderella watched the people dance and felt her heart leap. She listened to all the laughter and felt.. Almost normal. A handsome man touched her arm, asked her to dance. She didn't know how to dance but suddenly even that was alright. He smiled at her and she felt her heart leap.

It was the eldest stepsister who recognized her first and became very angry that the most popular boy in the whole school would dance with her. Cinderella was smiling when, from behind her, she heard her stepsister's voice calling her name. Terror crept into Cinderella's heart. She turned just in time to feel her stepsister yank her arm back until the frail blue cloth ripped, exposing her arms.

"I'm sorry," she said to the man dancing. "But she is a pretender. Look at her! She's not beautiful, she's a freak! I saw her, she does this--" she jerked Cinderella's scarred arm up for the crowd to see, "to herself! She's not beautiful, she's--she's..."

"She's broken," finished the Stepmother, walking up. "She will never be able to erase the scars, she will never be normal. She is useless, broken just like glass."

"No, I..." Cinderella wanted to tell the crowd, the boy, that that was all a lie. She wanted to tell them all that she wasn't a pretender. Her heart felt like stone. She was pretending. She didn't go to school here. This wasn't a dress bought at a store. And she wasn't like them. She was broken. She shook her head, tears falling from her eyes, and turned. She didn't stop running until she couldn't see the school anymore.

She ran into her room and grabbed the shard of glass she kept there. She was going to throw it away--but what did it matter, she was never going to change. The scars would never go away. She would never be normal. She probably didn't even have a home anymore.

She laid the glass against her skin, pushed, ready to slice it. But then she looked up. The stars were still there, still bright, still twinkling. Maybe she was broke....but you could glue pieces of a glass back together. She just needed to try. It hurt her to throw the glass away, as far as she could into the dark sky. But she wouldn't glue anything together again by running.

Cinderella took a deep, deep breath in and looked behind her, back toward the dance. Then she turned and took a chance, followed her heart and chased the twinkling stars: she went back to defend her name, her hope and her dreams. She and the handsome boy did not marry. But Cinderella never gave up trying. She never went back to the basement. She never cut herself again. She was stronger than that. She had broken away. She had taken a chance, dared to believe in the impossible.

And she won.

Tonight is Homecoming.

It's like one of the biggest nights in the school year. I didn't go last year. I thought it was kind of lame. I mean, it was just a football game, right? And I was a freshman so no one even knew I existed. My mom would have had to drive me. Or, God forbid, my dad. So I didn't go. The next day when everyone was talking about it, I pretended I had been there. I pretended an upper classman noticed me and asked me to go to the back of the bleachers and make out. But he didn't, really. And even if one had of, I probably would rather puke my guts up in front of the entire student body than make out with anyone, no matter how cute he might be. But not going to Homecoming is almost as bad as a Junior or Senior choosing not to go to Prom. It's like tattooing a big sign on your forehead that says LOSER. It would give the kids a reason to make fun of me for the next two years.

So I pretended I'd been there. I pretended I was cool and nobody could really prove I hadn't been there, so it kind of worked out. Except I knew I hadn't been there, which meant I still felt like a loser.

I don't want to have to feel that way again. And smart people learn from their mistakes. So I'm at Homecoming tonight.

It's been all anyone could talk about at school all week. Each day, there was a different theme. School Spirit Day, Character Day, Sixties Day, Rock and Roll Day and today was Duo Day. You and a friend were supposed to dress up as twins. Girlfriends and boyfriends dressed in matching colors. Some even made matching shirts. McKayla and Cason, the Homecoming Queen and King, each wore a red shirt. On McKayla's, the word "Queen" was emblazoned on the front; "King" was on Cason's. I saw one couple that had the same idea. Their shirts read: "Future Wife of Adam S" and "Future Husband of Katy W." Everybody had a twin. Everybody was so happy and excited. You could just feel the energy. Every time the bell rang and we all poured into the hallways, the noise level alone could have told you that something was different.

Everybody was happy.

Unless you're not a cheerleader or football player.

I think Homecoming was really created just for the cheerleaders and the football players. Just like how at Prom the Prom Queen will never be just a normal girl: it will always be one of those girls. The popular ones. The cheerleaders. The ones that barely scratch by academically but who are loved by everyone anyway. The Homecoming Court will never be made up of the quiet kids, the ones who do their work and sit by themselves at lunch. It's just not going to happen. And the thing is, because everyone loves that crowd, the popular one, the entire student body feels an obligation to like the same things they do. It doesn't matter if you think dressing up like a sixties hippie is stupid…. You'll do it so that you can pretend you 'fit in' with the rest of them. It doesn't matter if you know with one hundred percent certainty nobody is going to ask you onto the floor at the Homecoming Dance…. You're still going to go so that you can pretend to be normal. You will do what you have to do to feel like you fit in.

At least, I will.

So, I'm sitting in the bleachers, watching a stupid game. All I know is that my school color is red so the guys on the field in red uniforms are part of my school. People have their faces painted red and are all waving red and white pom poms. The stadium lights are so bright that even I can see everything on the field, even sitting way up high in the bleachers. I have no idea who is winning because I don't understand the game. All I know is that boys keep jumping on each other and everyone goes wild when they do it. Mostly, I'm watching the other kids, the ones not on the field. Boys have their hands in the back pockets of their girlfriends' jeans. Girls are hugging each other and laughing. Others are eating hot dogs and popcorn. A lot are loudly cheering on the team.

It's going to be a long night. The Homecoming dance is in the gym, after the game. I told my mother I really wanted to go. So she isn't coming to get me until midnight. That's, like, four hours away. And the dance will be just as bad as this game except I'll be watching my classmates dance. The October wind is brisk. I hunch my shoulders and stand. I make my way down the bleachers. I have to go to the bathroom. I see a couple under the bleachers making out and I wonder if they'll be stopped by a passing teacher. I think about how I could ruin their night by going to tell a teacher what they are doing, and where they are. If everybody isn't having fun, why should they? But I know I won't. They'd just go somewhere else.

The school hallways are deserted. Teachers are still setting up the gym for the dance; I can hear people in there. I walk into the restroom but instead of going into one of the stalls, I brace my hands on the sink and lean forward, staring at myself in the mirror. I tell myself it's not that bad, that it will be over soon. I feel like I should hurry back out there, but then I ask myself why. No one is looking for me. No one even knows I'm here. Back outside again, I head back up to the football field. But I don't get far when I hear laughter. I turn in the direction of it and walk to the side of the school. Partially hidden under a big weeping willow tree sit five kids. Two girls and three boys. I know the names of the two girls and one of the guys, but I've never seen the other guy. He must be popular, though, because the other three are.

Both of the girls are on Student Council.

I start to walk away but when I step on a branch, they hear me. The guy whose name is Derrick sees me first. "Hey! Hey, come on over here. What's your name again?"

I hesitate but then slowly head closer. They are sitting in a circle so I don't see the bottle until I am almost up to them.

"Taya," I answer.

"That's right, Taya. How're you doing'? You want to play with us? We need another girl."

The girls laugh and nod. "Yeah, Taya, come on. Join us. Have you ever played before?" Jessica is one of the most popular girls in school. I have no idea why she is not down on the football field with the other popular girls are. But if one of the most popular girls in schools asks you to join her, you'd have to be pretty stupid to say no. So I shrug, trying to act like I can't make up my mind, and walk closer. The boys scoot closer together to make room for me.

"Have you ever played?" Jessica asked again, pushing her blonde hair out of her eyes. I smell alcohol on her breath. I swallow but shake my head, telling the truth for once.

Derrick takes the bottle that's lying in the middle of the circle and hands it to me. "No problem. All you got to do is spin it. Whoever it lands on, you have to kiss."

Warning bells go off in my head. I know I don't want to play this game. But I can't just get up and leave after I told them I'd play. They'd think I was weird or something. I stay put, but shake my head. "That's okay, I'll go last." I say. Derrick shrugs and takes the bottle himself. He spins it and it lands on Amber. Laughing, Amber looks at Jessica, then shrugs and gives Derrick a kiss on the mouth. I lower my eyes to the ground, my stomach churning. Amber gets to spin next. It lands on Jessica. They kiss. The knot in my stomach gets worse and I hunch my shoulders, while I'm trying to think of a way out of this game that wouldn't make me look like a complete idiot. Or, worse, childish.

It's finally my turn. I don't know why, but I go ahead and spin the bottle. I feel like throwing up while it's turning. Everybody is cheering. Finally, the bottle stops. It is pointing toward the boy whose name I don't even know. Everybody laughs.

"Pucker up, Nick!" Derrick laughs.

Nick. His name is Nick.

My face is flaming hot when I look up at him. Nick is actually really cute. He's got amber colored hair, and a whole bunch of it. He's got dark brown eyes that have little gold specks in them. He's hot. But that's beside the point. There is no way I can kiss him.

"What are you waitin' on?" Amber asks.

"Go on, do it." Jessica prods.

Nick smiles. He knows I don't want to kiss him. The challenge I sense in his eyes makes me lean over. I kiss his cheek; sit back. Everybody explodes with laughter. Even Nick laughs. Derrick holds the bottle up. "If you don't give him a real kiss, Taya, you have to drink a shot of this. And it's Jack Daniels. You probably want to kiss him." I didn't even notice, until he said that, the two shot glasses sitting on the ground. I'd rather drink a shot of pure alcohol than kiss anybody. So, without looking at Nick, I say bravely: "I can drink it."

"Have you ever had a drink, Taya?" Amber asks. Her breath is clean.

I nod, lying, and reaching over for the shot glass. Derrick pours it to the top. "You gotta drink it in one gulp. No little sips."

I don't even think about the alcohol. All

I'm thinking about is that this is my ticket out of this game. If I get drunk, so what? I'll have a really bad headache tomorrow morning. My mom will ground me forever when she smells my breath. I'll throw up. But it's not as bad as kissing someone. I just chug it. It burns a path down my throat and my eyes sting with tears almost immediately. Choking, I put the shot glass down on the ground and shake my head, trying to clear it. I hear everyone laughing again, but it feels like I'm under water. Thankfully, no one's bottle lands on me. When it's my turn again, I choose to drink another shot. My stomach starts feeling a little woozy after the second shot but it doesn't really feel that bad. This time around, I'm not so lucky. Nick's bottle lands on me. He smiles at me. "I'm not drinking it," he announced boldly. Before I understand what he's about to do, he leans over and pushes his mouth against mine. Maybe it's the alcohol that I've had. Maybe it's because it happened so fast. I don't know why, but I don't stop him. I don't feel anything though. He doesn't put his tongue in my mouth, just a quick push of his lips to mine. Then it's my turn. My bottle lands on Amber. I drink another shot. And so it goes. Derrick chooses to drink a shot instead of having to kiss me. He is drunk too.

This really is a fun game, once you start to loosen up. I laugh a lot over the next hour. I don't remember how many people I kissed. I don't remember how many kissed me. I know I drank more than I kissed. I drank more than anybody else. Once the bottle was empty, the game turned. Now, instead of drinking a shot, if you refuse to kiss somebody, Derrick said you have to remove a piece of clothing. The girls thought this was hilarious. And I don't think it was that bad a deal. I mean, it's better than kissing someone, right?

For the first time in my life, I feel like I truly fit in. I feel like they are my friends and we're all just playing a game. I don't feel like the outsider. I am the outsider, though. When my bottle lands on Jessica, I choose to remove my shoes instead of kissing her. Nick, also drunk, gets into the spirit of things and removes his tie. I don't know how many rounds we play until the only thing left for me to remove is my skirt and shirt. I don't want to remove them, and I don't want to kiss either. But Derrick said, "Last round, Taya. Own it up. Just flash us, then we'll call it quits."

So I do. I don't take my shirt off, but I pull
it up. I have a tank top on, so I don't have a bra.
I'm not even embarrassed; it's just funny,
because of the alcohol. I feel really sick then
and stand to go to the bathroom. But I can't
walk real good. I fall a few steps later and puke
my guts out on the school lawn. Then I stumble
a couple steps more and lay down. Minutes
later, I'm asleep.

***** ***** *****

I wake up cold. My head is killing me,
it's not spinning anymore, but it is throbbing in
pain. I put the heel of my palm against my right
eye and push real hard. The pressure helps my
head a little. I call for Nick, or Derrick; then for
Jessica or Amber. But I don't hear anything. I
stand up and look toward the football field. The
field lights are off. That means the game is over.
Everybody must be in the gym at the dance.
Still holding the side of my head with my palm,
I walk into the school. But instead of going into

the gym right away, I go for the bathroom. The bright lights make my head hurt even more. I squint my eyes and head for one of the stalls. It's not until I come out to wash my hands that I see myself in the mirror. Puke is on my shirt. My hair is awful, tangled and matted. Leaves are in it too. I get a paper towel and try to clean myself up some. I take my hair down and use my fingers as a comb. Then I put it back up. It looks a little better, but not much. I wish I had a toothbrush. I've got an awful taste in my mouth. Then I reach into my pocket book and pull out my phone. It's eleven thirty. My mom will be outside to pick me up in half an hour. I've missed most of the dance. I'm hungry and I feel terrible.

Food will be in the gym.

I leave the bathroom and walk into the gym. The noise level makes my head worse right away. A huge, silver disco ball hangs from the ceiling. Loud music is being played and everybody is on the floor. I walk over to the food table and start to get some punch. Then I realize it's probably been spiked. I get a water bottle from a cooler instead, and a few cookies. Then I make my way into the darkest corner I can find and lean against the wall. Yup, that's me: the wallflower.

I'm staring at the dance floor without really seeing anything. But something is different. Everybody keeps looking at me. When I go back to the food table to get a few more cookies, a couple of girls start snickering at me and then they walk away. Even some people on the dance floor are looking at me weird. Jessica and Derrick walk by. I say hello but they ignore me, like they didn't just play a game with me an hour or two ago. I walk out of the gym and lean against the wall. I slide down it until I'm sitting with my knees pulled up to my chin. I don't look up when I hear a couple girls whisper, "There she is," as they walk right past me. I don't even notice the tears that creep from nowhere into my eyes and roll down my cheek. I'm not sure why yet, but I know for sure that this is one of the worst nights of my life.

Today's been super weird at school. I can't go in any class without somebody laughing at me, pointing or snickering.

I've never really been bullied. I've never really been picked on. I've just been ignored. Like nobody even knew I was there kind of ignored. Last year, two weeks before the end of the school year, my math teacher did not even know my name. My math teacher did not know my name after a full year of seeing me every day in class and grading papers with my name on them. That's how ... dull ... I am. That's how much I've been ignored. I mean, when the teacher doesn't even know your name, you don't have much luck of anyone else knowing you exist on the planet. And it's not like I just think he didn't know my name, he truly didn't. I know that for a fact because I went up to his desk and asked him if I could have my homework that he'd already graded back. He started looking through the stack of papers on his desk and then scratched his head, looked at me and asked me my name.

So, like I said, I'm ignored.

That's why when a lot of people are laughing at me, I notice it right away.

I have no idea why they're laughing. Maybe there's something wrong with my outfit. It's possible I came to school with my shoes on the wrong feet. But no, when I look, my shoes are on right, my shirt is buttoned straight and there's nothing I can find on my face. No granola bar crumbles leftover from my breakfast sticking to the corner of my mouth. I don't have any zits. I have no idea why they're all looking at me weird. But they definitely are. On the way to my English class, I pass two girls standing in the hall. As I walk past, they both stop talking and stare at me. I want to ask them why, but I don't. Instead, I just walk right past them, pretending I don't care. I'm good at pretending but it gets harder to ignore when I hear one of them whisper, "Freak."

Maybe one of them saw some of my scars somehow.

I mean, at Homecoming, I did have a

tank top on. I wore a sweater over it, but maybe the sleeves were rolled up and somebody saw the scars? I don't remember rolling the sleeves up, though. I shake my head to clear it as I grab the only left-handed desk in the class and pull it to the front row. I always sit in the front row, because it keeps me out of the line of fire from the other kids, but there aren't many left handed desks. Like, in the whole school. Most of my classes don't have even one. It's not a big deal, I've gotten used to writing on the right handed desks, but I always make sure to grab the left handed desks in the two classes that have one. It makes me feel normal, sitting in a desk that was intended for people like me.

Before you judge me for being left-handed, did you know that Albert Einstein was left handed? Obama is a leftie too. Yeah, so was Osama bin Laden, but that doesn't really mean anything. I mean, there are lots of really famous good people who were left handed. They say that being left handed means I'm more creative. They're wrong about that. I'm definitely not creative. I can't even draw a straight line. I don't sing or play instruments either. Some of the kids in English write really cool poems. Not me. I'm not creative, but I am clumsy. And that's another trait of left handed people. Being clumsy. Like, I trip over shoelaces all the time. And I wasn't kidding when I said it was possible I came to school with my shoes on the wrong feet. I'm fifteen years old and still have to really think hard about which shoe goes on which foot.

It's almost like God said, "You're going to be left handed so that you'll never forget how weird you really are." It's just one more thing in a list of long things that make me different from the other kids in class. And, I mean, there have been kids who were just bored and made me have a bad year. Like, one time, there was this girl who always pinched me whenever we stood in line so that I would let her cut in front of me without telling. That was back in, like, the second grade. So it's been awhile since kids picked on me. Usually, they just ignore me. I've gotten used to being ignored.

They aren't ignoring me today.

They're laughing at me.

I just don't know why.

We have to give an oral book report today in English. I hate giving oral book reports because I hate being in front of the class. It makes me feel like I'm sticking out like a sore thumb. Sometimes Mrs. Simmons' cool ideas take too much work. Some of her ideas are cool to write about, but not talk about. I start off pretty good, though. I'm not super talented at writing anything but I'm also not terrible. I understand grammar and can usually come up with a way to say what I want to say. I don't like giving reports, but I can do it. That is, until I realize that the kids in the class aren't listening to anything I say. Instead, they're laughing at me again. Covering their mouths with the palms of their hands and looking at each other like they know a secret I don't know. Which is probably true. It bothers me, seeing them laugh at me. I wish I knew what was wrong. I mumble my way through the rest of the report, and then slump down in my chair.

"Hey, Taya, that was pretty lame. I mean, now that we know how interesting you can be and all." Trey whispers from behind me. The fact that Trey is laughing at me says a lot. Trey has never laughed at me. Not all year long. He's a goofball, and a smartass, but he doesn't make fun of people. I look over my shoulder to see him laughing.

"What are you talking about?" I whisper.

"Nothin'," he smirked.

Angry, I face the front again and let some of my hair fall over my cheek to hide it. It is burning red.

By the time lunch rolls around, I just want to go home. It's been a terrible day. I'm pretty sure that somebody, somehow, saw my scars and told all the other kids that I'm cut up or something. I don't know what else it could be. And they are ugly. My scars. I mean, do you know anybody that cuts their own skin? I tug my sleeves down until my fingers grab it and hold it over my palm, to make sure they don't accidentally slide up or something. It's been really hard to pretend not to hear the whispers. They are being so mean. I bet I've a dozen stupid comments all day, comments like, "she's just a trashy freak" and when I went into the bathroom, these girls gathered up their makeup and headed out, saying, "My mom says it can rub off on you, you know. Bad character."

Bad character. Me, the girl who has never been on a date? What?

I go through the lunch line, get my tray of food and then look for an empty table. The lunchroom is crowded. I don't see an empty table. So I just sit down at the far end of one of the long tables, the ones that can hold almost twenty kids. I don't know anybody at the table, so I think I'll be alright. I hear everyone talking. I hear everyone laughing. But all I can think about are the girls in the bathroom. They thought I was some sort of plague, or something. They couldn't wait to get away from me.

I don't know why, but I look up. I see Derrick and Jessica standing in the lunch line. Derrick has his phone and he's showing it to some guy I'd never met. Jessica is looking around the cafeteria, like she's looking for me. All three are laughing. For the first time, I think of the spin the bottle game. A sick feeling creeps up over me, making a big knot form in the middle of my stomach. All of a sudden, the noise of the cafeteria fades away until I can't hear anything but the roaring in my head. I am mad. I am so mad I can't see straight. I don't know how I know, but suddenly I know that my scars have nothing to do with why everybody's treating me funny. I know it has to do with that stupid game. I don't think about getting up but, all of a sudden, I feel myself moving toward the lunch line. Jessica sees me coming, she nudges Derrick. But he doesn't care. He just grins at me and nods his head.

"Hey, Taya."

I don't say hello. I just reach over and grab his phone. I jerk it out of his hand and look at the screen. It's not until I look at it that my whole world stops. It's a picture of me. I'm standing under the willow tree and I've got this big stupid smile on my face. My hands are holding my shirt, and it's pulled up. All the way up. My small, white breasts are right there. I feel my face burning up; throw up is in my throat. He took a picture. Of course he took a picture. I just don't remember it. I don't remember a lot. Because I was drunk. Because I wanted to fit in. Because they made me feel like I fit in. I drop the phone. It crashes to the floor and I hear Derrick warning me I was going to have to pay if his phone was broken. But what about my life? Who was going to have to pay for it being broken?

I turn and run. I run out of the cafeteria. Our school is huge. It's got two buildings. The two buildings are attached by a walkway. The kids call this walkway the "smoking porch" because it's where all the kids go to smoke between breaks. I don't smoke, but it is the closest place I can go to get away. I run outside and then duck between a column and the side of the building. It's a tight squeeze; no one will ever know I'm here. I slide down until my bottom touches the ground, bury my face in my knees and cry.

Probably a thousand kids laughed at me today. Probably every one of them has seen that picture. Why would he do that? Why would anybody do that? I thought we were friends. I thought I was one of them, and that we were just having fun. I was so stupid. I was so, so stupid. There's a razor in my locker. I think about it, its pink grip and shiny blade. I need it. It's the only thing that will stop this feeling. But to get it, I'd have to go inside to the lockers. The lockers are next to the cafeteria and everybody in there just saw me run out. Going back now would be suicide. So instead, I use my fingernails to scratch at my wrists. I scratch my right wrist until it bleeds. But I still don't feel better.

I am embarrassed. Why did I flash them? Why did they ask me to?

I skip all my other classes. I don't move from the smoking porch. I hear the kids come out, laugh, and go. But they don't see me. I stay still and just hide. I've missed a couple of tests today. I don't care. I don't care about anything, except getting home. When the final bell rings, I have to get up. If I don't, I'll miss my bus and then I won't be able to get home until after five when my mom gets off work.

I don't even notice the other kids on the bus. I don't even know if they laughed at me or not. I don't really see anything. I don't hear anything. It's like I'm in a tunnel. When I get home, I go to my room. I get the blade out... but I am too tired now, after crying all day. I just lay it down on the desk and get in bed. I just want to sleep.

***** ***** *****

The next week of school is more of the same. It doesn't stop. I'm called awful names like "whore" and "trash" and "slut." Twice today, two different guys have come up and offered me five dollars to flash them. I almost spit in their faces but then I thought that would just give everybody even more reason to talk about me, so I don't. I just turn and walk away. Their laughter haunts me. I hear it everywhere.

Jessica, Amber, Derrick and Nick act like they've never seen me before in their lives. Nobody seems to care that they were drunk too. Because they weren't the ones who flashed the whole school. Trey tries to be nice. He talked to me today, told me he still likes me. He's the only one who does. He also told me what happened. Derrick sent the picture to his friends, and they sent it to theirs and that's how the whole school knows how small my breasts are. That's why the whole school knows that my right breast is just a little bit bigger than my left. That's why the whole school knows that I have cuts on my stomach too. Or maybe they don't. Because they were looking at my breasts instead.

My whole high school experience is ruined because of this. Nobody will ever forget this. I mean, how could they: they have a picture to remind them. I fail two big tests. I forget to turn in another English assignment, and I make a D on a History project. All in one week. In Mrs. Simmon's class, we are reading The Scarlet Letter. I feel like her. I feel like there is a huge red stamp on my forehead that says "STUPID FREAK." There's nothing I could do that would get the red stamp off. It's there forever. I can't undo it. I can't make everybody understand. There is no reason that would justify what I did. There's nothing that will make it ok.

My whole life is ruined.

Pink is on the radio singing "Raise
your glass, if you are wrong in all the right ways,
All my underdogs, come on, come, We will
never ever be anything but loud and nitty gritty,
dirty little freaks." My mom is not home right
now, so I can turn it up as loud as I want. It's so
loud I can't hear myself think, which is the
point. I just got home from another sucky day
at school where everybody laughed their butts
off at my naked self. Trey tried to talk to me but
I think he just feels weird since he's sitting
behind me for an hour. He doesn't want to be
too obvious that he's laughing his butt off along
with the rest of them. The music is so loud that
all I can feel is the vibrating beat of the drum
when the knife slices my wrist. I don't feel like
carving anything right now. I just want it cut.
It bleeds and then I stop it. Before I do, though,
I look at the blood spilling out. How much
would I have to lose in order to die? My whole
body is filled with blood; I'd have to lose a lot
probably in order to die. I'd either have to make
a really, really deep cut or just not stop it. But if
I didn't stop it, it would take a really, really long

time and it would be really messy. I wouldn't want to leave a big mess. Thinking about dying makes me nervous. I quickly grab the towel from under my bed and stop the flow of crimson.

I sing out loud with the song. My favorite part is that one line, the "we will never be anything but loud and nitty, gritty dirty little freaks." Even though it says the word "dirty," somehow it makes being a freak sound like a cool thing. Those are the best types of songs, the kind that makes it seem like being different is a good thing. Lots of people say that, but no one really believes it. Really, everyone wants to be just like everyone else. Being different means sticking out in a crowd and nobody really wants to stick out in a crowd. I don't feel awesome when I hear someone call me a freak at school, not the first time they say it and not the hundredth time either. But when Pink sings about it being cool to be different, well, it just sounds better. She says I can choose to let it go. I don't know how to do that though. How am I supposed to just keep pretending they aren't talking about me? I'm not just treated like the fool, I am the fool. After all, nobody made me do the flash dance.

The song goes off and I shut the music off. I feel like I'm going to burst if I don't do something. I gotta get out of here. I gotta go somewhere, do something. If I don't, I'm going to cut again and my wrist is sore and I don't like cutting on my stomach. I leave the bedroom and race down the stairs. I walk outside and take off down the street. There's a park about a block away, I'll go there. It's not a big park so sometimes there aren't a lot of people there, and I can just chill and think

I'm lucky today. There's nobody at the park. I sit on the swings and push myself. I get really high. It's kind of like the music, it drowns everything else out. When I was little, I used to pretend I was flying. It still kind of feels like that. The only difference is that now I'm not going anywhere. I used to pretend I was flying to a mystical world that had a different name every time I sat on a swing. Now, it feels like I'm falling.

I don't see him at first. Not until I finally slow swinging. He is walking toward me. He is too far away for me to be sure who he is. When I realize it's Nick, my heart starts pounding like crazy. I don't know whether to try and punch him in the nose or run away. He didn't take the picture.... But he didn't stop Derrick from spreading it either. And I'm seen him laughing. When he sees me on the swing, I see him stop walking. I wonder if he'll just turn and leave. But he doesn't. He walks closer. Neither of us says anything for a long time. I stare at the ground; he sits in the swing next to me and pushes himself slowly, dragging his feet on the mulch.

"Hi."

I don't answer him. I just keep looking at the ground.

"I guess you're pretty mad at me."

I turn my head to look at him and catch him looking at me. I look away, then shrug. "You didn't the picture."

"No." He mumbles. Then, "So, I didn't know you live around here."

I shrug. "About a block away. Do you live near here?"

"Not really, no. But my cousin does." He shrugs. "I was supposed to be hanging out with him this afternoon. But he got detention and won't be out for another hour or so."

I look away and don't say anything.

We sit in silence for what seems like forever. It is really awkward. I can't really just get up and leave, because I know he would think it's rude. And I don't know what to say about Homecoming, or the picture. I actually just kind of wish I could forget about that whole night, but that's hard to do with Nick sitting beside me.

"So…"

I look over at him and see him pushing his foot against the gravel again. Then he looks up at me.

"I just want you to know that, like, I didn't know Derrick was going to do anything with the picture. I don't even know why he took it."

I shrug, look down at the ground. After a

moment, I look back up at him. "Did he send it to you?"

He nodded. "Yeah. But, like, I deleted it. I didn't send it to nobody."

"That's because everybody already had it."

He looked away. After a long minute, he looked back. "I don't know, Taya. I'm glad you're here, though. I been wanting to talk to you, but it's kind of hard to do that right now at school."

I don't say anything.

"I mean, I just really like you."

That comes as a really big surprise. I don't know what to think about that. I don't whether or not to believe him. I don't know why he would like me. Or maybe I do. Maybe he likes me because I flashed him my breasts.

He squints one eye and says, "I'm sorry for having a part in it all. But I would like to make it up to you. Maybe we can hang out every once in awhile?"

"At school?"

He hesitates. "Well, I don't know about at school. It's not that I would be ashamed or anything like that, though. It's just that the guys would give me a real hard time about it. Maybe we could keep it a secret, you know? It's nice to have something that nobody else knows about."

"When would we hang out? Where?"

Nick shrugs. "I don't know. The park's a good place. You said you don't live far from here; maybe I could come by your place sometime. Or we could walk to the Moby's theater for a movie, it's not far."

"Are you saying this because I flashed everybody?"

"No."

I don't know why. Maybe it's because of the horrified look on his face. Maybe it's because he's got one eye squinted. Maybe it's because he's just really cute. I don't know why, but I believe him. A warm little feeling comes over me, creeps into my stomach and makes me happy. Somebody likes me. And somebody cute too. Maybe it all really is going to be okay.

"Okay. Maybe we can hang out sometimes."

He smiles at me. He's got a beautiful smile, really big with pretty white teeth. He gets up and starts to push me on the swing. I haven't had anybody push me on the swings in forever. It makes me relax and feel a little better. It's not so awkward anymore. He tells me he knows how to play a game called Dead Man. He helps me lay across two swings, my head and shoulders in one, my feet in another, and then he swings me. It feels really weird. And free. I feel free for the first time in a very long time. I feel like I'm flying again. This time, though, maybe I am going somewhere after all. Maybe there's more to flying than just falling.

He stays with me at the park for almost an hour before he says he has to get back. His cousin will be getting home soon. He gives me a hug. It's been a really long time since I've had a hug. He feels skinnier than I thought he was. The hug is real quick but it makes me feel good. I almost don't even remember the kids at school and all the mean things they say. I almost don't even care right now that I flashed everybody and Derrick took a picture of it. I almost don't even care. It only takes one person, just one, to make me feel better about everything. It only takes Nick.

***** ***** *****

It's been two weeks since me and Nick started hanging out. We hang out at least a couple days a week. It's a little weird because he doesn't want me telling anybody at school that we hang out. But I guess he's just trying to keep all his friends there too. Nobody would want to talk to him anymore if they knew he likes me. He took Ashley out on a date the other night. I got really mad about that but he told me about it first. He said that it was just a friend date and that nothing would happen. He said it was just so that everybody would think he hadn't changed. He hasn't even kissed me yet, so I kind of believe that he just likes hanging out with people. In a way, I'm glad that he hasn't kissed me. I think that's kind of gross. It makes me think of my dad and I'm pretty sure I'm not supposed to think of my dad when I kiss somebody else. But there's this little part of me that wishes Nick would kiss me. It would make me believe that he really likes me, since nobody would kiss someone he didn't like.

The kids at school are still being nasty to me.

Today has been the worst day ever.

Nicole's mom found out about the picture. Nicole is in all of my classes. Sometimes she's kind of nice. She usually doesn't make fun of me or anything. She's kind of quiet and shy. It says a lot that even Nicole has seen the picture because, usually, she doesn't get into all the gossip. But somebody texted the picture so she could see it too and her mom found it on her phone. Her mom went off the deep end. She called the school and yelled at the principal for allowing his students to pass trash around like that. So now I'm sitting in the principal's office, waiting to be yelled at. My mom is on the way too. I'm probably going to be expelled. Or at least suspended. I wish Nick were here. He would smile at me and make me feel like it's no big deal. But he's not. So instead I stare at the office and watch the other teenagers fidget in the chairs while they wait too. Some of them are sick and are waiting to go home. Some are waiting to talk to the principal like me. Some of them are signing into school after coming in late. It's a busy office.

"Taya?" Mr. Jordan's voice is real deep and low. I stand up and follow him into his office. It has a desk and a bookshelf. It's not real big, but it looks like a nice office. Awards and certificates hang on the wall.

"Taya, do you know why you're in my office?"

I nod.

"Why?"

"Nicole said her mom saw the picture and called you."

"That's right. Can you explain the picture, please? Why would you do something like that? And who took the picture?"

"Derrick took the picture," I mumbled, looking down at my hands. I use my finger to rub the scars on my wrist. I think about the knife at home.

"Why would you do something like that?" Mr. Jordan asks, frowning.

I shrug. "They asked me to."

Mr. Jordan sighs. "Taya, I know how smart you are. If your friends asked you to jump off a bridge, would you do that too? "

I know better than to say so but the real answer is, I just might. When you want friends, you will do anything to get them. But I bet Mr. Jordan never had that problem in school. I bet he was one of the popular boys and never had to do anything he didn't want to so he could be part of a group. So he wouldn't have a clue. Instead of telling him that, though, I just shrug and look down at my fingernails. Red paint is chipped on all but two of the nails. I use my fingers to cover up a nail. Mr. Jordan spends the next twenty minutes chewing me out, telling me that my reputation is not something to take lightly. He says I need to learn more about decorum and tells me I have to write an essay on what that word means tonight. He tells me that since it all happened outside of school hours, he cannot give me detention but warns me that if he sees anything else like that from me, he will. He's called my mom because it's the right thing to do, telling her about the picture. I don't say anything. I feel my face turning hot. I have never liked getting in trouble. And, I mean, yeah, I shouldn't have flashed them... but they shouldn't have taken the picture of it, or sent it to others. I thought I was with friends and they betrayed that. But does anybody chew their butts out for that? Nope. Just mine.

My mother is one of the prettiest women I've ever seen. All the kids at school say so. At least they did, before I became the school slut. She's got the same color hair I do, blonde, except hers is a lot longer and a lot more blonde. Mine is dirty blonde. Naturally. Anyway, she's also got the biggest pair of blue eyes you've ever seen. Mine are amber brown and narrow. On Asian girls, this is really pretty. On me, it looks like I'm squinting into the bright sun all the time. Mom's got real high cheekbones too and she still looks like she's in her twenties, even though she's not. It's hard being her daughter, actually, because I'm always being compared to her and, except for the fact that we both have blonde hair and we're both short, we look nothing alike. I tell you all this because when Mom gets mad, it shows on every line of her beautiful face. Her usually thick lips purse together so hard they become almost invisible. She sucks in her cheeks too, which must be really hard to do since her lips are pursed so tightly together. It turns her beautiful face into a picture of fury so strong that even if you had never seen Mom before, you'd instantly know she was pissed off if you walked in while she was mad. I know I'm in trouble when she jerks the door to the school office open and I see her face. Her lips are pursed, her cheeks are sucked in and her eyes are blazing red hot lava. I slink in the chair and lower my eyes to the ground in an effort to avoid the wrath I know is coming.

Instead of looking at me, though, she looks at the secretary. "Mr. Jordan called me to come in. About that child," she says and, without even turning to look at me, points one finger behind her back toward me. The secretary nods, tells her to have a seat and picks up the phone to call Mr. Jordan.

"Mom," I say tentatively.

She does not answer me. She does not even turn around to look at me. I sigh and give up, slink down in the chair again and keep my eyes on the floor. Mr. Jordan opens his door and ushers her inside.

I am told to wait.

They are in there forever. I have no idea what's being said. I can guess, though. I try to think about Nick. The other day, while we were hanging out, he said I was beautiful. Nobody has ever called me beautiful. He said he has a surprise for me on Saturday, he said it's a big one. I'm supposed to see him this afternoon which means it sucks that I'm probably going to get grounded for life on the way home. Nick says he never gets grounded. He says he almost never sees his parents. Their divorced and so his mom works two jobs to take care of him. And his dad moved to another state so he doesn't get to see him much anymore. I wish my dad would move to another state.

Finally, Mr. Jordan's door opens. Mom

walks out. Her lips are pursed, but she's not sucking in her cheeks anymore. Maybe that's a good sign. She calls my name and I stand up. She doesn't say goodbye to the secretary, she just walks out the door. I'm expected to follow. I do and it's totally silent in the car. Mom and I are pretty tight. Getting in trouble with her makes me feel like I've really messed up. I stare out the window and watch the cars pass. It's not until she turns out of the school parking lot that I hear her exhale harshly. I look toward her from the corner of my eye. She's got her elbow propped on the windowsill and the side of her head in her hand. She looks almost sad. That makes me feel even worse.

"I'm sorry," I mumble.

She says nothing for a long time before, "What *in the hell* were you thinking?"

I shrug. "I just… I don't know. I guess I was drunk."

"You guess? I tell you, Taya, I hope to God you were because if you did that sober, we have really big problems."

Silence.

"What I don't get is how you could have thought doing something so stupid was okay, even if you were drunk." Before I can say anything, she adds, "And when, pray tell, did you become an alcoholic?"

"Mom, I'm not—"

"So is that why you wanted to go to

Homecoming? To get drunk with your boyfriends?"

"I—"

"What else did you do that night?"

"Nothing, we just played the game–"

"What game?"

"Spin the Bottle."

"Good God."

"Mom, I don't drink."

"You just told me you were drunk."

"I *was* drunk. I got drunk because I had never drank anything before and they asked me to and –"

She won't let me talk. She keeps interrupting me.

"You think I'm going to believe that you've never had a drink before? Girls that don't drink, Taya, *do not* raise their shirts in front of boys."

"I did drink, but that was just the first time and ---"

"Did you do it because you like one of them?"

"I did it because they asked me to. They told me it would be the last round of the game and I was tired and didn't want to drink no more—"

"Then why in God's name did you not just get the hell out of there?"

Silence. I sigh heavily and look out the window. If she won't let me finish, she won't ever understand.

"I just wanted some friends, Mom."

"You sure know how to pick them, don't you?"

"You're not going to understand."

"I don't have to understand, Taya, because there is a picture of you without a shirt on! What else is there to understand? Don't you get that this is the reputation you're going to have for the *rest of your life?* Don't you understand that the boys that see that picture are going to think you put out more a picture?"

My face turns red. "I don't ever—"

"What if he said that if you didn't, he wouldn't be your friend? Would you then, Taya?"

Tears sting my eyes and a picture of Nick flashes in my mind. He said I was beautiful. He didn't try to kiss me. What if he did? What if he told me he wouldn't be my boyfriend anymore if I wouldn't kiss him? Is that why he took the other girl out on a date? Because she'll kiss him?

"And if you don't care about your reputation, then maybe you should remember that the way you act when you're not at home reflects on *my* reputation. And your dad's. And I do care about the way people see me because I was raised to be a lady."

"I'm sorry! Okay, I am sorry! God, I'm sorry for everything I've ever done that's not been perfect! I'm sorry I was even born, if I hadn't been, then you wouldn't have anything to worry about."

I think she's going to slap me. Her fingers curl in on the steering wheel and she slams on the brake. My hand goes out to the dashboard automatically as I'm jerked forward in the seat. She doesn't say anything for a long time. We pull into the driveway and she turns the car off. I go to open my door but her fingers lock around my wrist tightly. I look back at her.

"If I get another phone call like that, Taya, so help me God, I will lock you in your room and then I will...." She clicked her teeth together and closed her eyes, trying to get a grip on her temper.

"You'll what? Kill me? Maybe I should just save you the trouble and do it myself." I jerk my hand out of her grasp, jump out of the car and slam the door shut. I hear her yell my name but I ignore her and go into the house. I run up to my room and lock the bedroom door behind me. I'm so angry I feel the blood rushing to my head. I start to get the razor but there's too much energy in me. I might actually do it, cut the hell out of my wrist. Instead, I grab the pillow off my bed and throw it against the wall, then fall down against the wall on the floor. I hide my face in my knees and pretend I'm not crying. I wish Mom knew that the kids at school have already told me everything she did. I wish

she knew they called me awful names, that I
don't have any friends for real. I wish she knew.
But I don't know how to tell her. I don't know
how to make her understand how hard it is in
that place. I wish she wasn't so stressed out all
the time so I could maybe talk to her without
feeling like I was going to set off a volcano.

I wish.

I hear my phone ringing in the book bag
I dropped on the bed. At first, I don't care, but it
might be Nick. So I get up, pull it out and open
it up to see Nick's number.

"Hello?"

"Hey, hey."

"Hi." I mumble.

"You don't sound so good."

"No. Mr. Jordan called my mom about
the picture."

"Oh." He's quiet for a minute before,
"Well, maybe I can cheer you up. You think we
can still meet up?"

"I don't know. I don't think she's going
to let me leave."

"Oh. Well, that's ok. I can't talk long
right now. But you wanna chat later?"

"Ok."

We do this every night. We get on instant
messenger and spent an hour or two chatting.
It's really cool. Or at least it has been. The last
two nights, the chats have gotten a little crazy.

Like, last night, he told me he'd dreamed about kissing me. He told me he dreamed I tasted sweet. It kind of made me a little worried but, like, it also made me feel... beautiful... so I didn't stop him. Maybe tonight he'll go back to just talking about school and how he's trying to get a job as a server at Burger King.

I spend the rest of the afternoon waiting for nine o clock to come. That's when he always gets on instant messenger. It helps keep me from cutting. It also helps keep me from thinking about the fight with Mom. It's nice to, you know, have something good to look forward to. Before Nick came along that day at the park, I didn't have anything good to look forward to. Today is only Tuesday. He said he can't give me the surprise until Saturday. That's a really long time to wait. I wonder if I can get him to tell me a hint tonight when we chat.

He gets on right at nine. We chat for a while. He tells me about hanging out with his friends. Him and Derrick are still good friends. That bothers me, but I don't want him to think I'm trying to tell him who he can be friends with and not so I don't tell him I wish he wouldn't hang around Derrick anymore. Sometimes I can't help but wonder if they talk about me like the other kids. But then he starts telling jokes. Nick loves to tell jokes. He tells a funny one about three brothers. I send him an "LOL" message and I really am smiling when he writes:

I got something to tell you.

    You do?

    Yeah. But it's kind of, like, hard to say. Can you give me something if I tell it to you?

    Give you what?

    I don't know. Do you ever think about kissing me?

I don't know what to write to that. I don't think about kissing nobody. Kissing is something really, really big in my life. It makes me think of my dad, even just the word. I can't imagine trying to kiss anybody else. But.... But if I did kiss Nick.... What would that be like? I think about it for a minute, and then write back: *Yea. Sometimes.*

    Have you ever kissed anybody?

I tell him the truth. *My dad.*

    LOL. Well that don't count. Nobody else?

    No.

    Cool. So when you think about it, what do you think it'd be like?

    I don't know. Sweet I guess.

    Yea. Kissing you would be sweet.

    What were you going to tell me?

He doesn't write back for a long time. Then the message pop on the screen and my heart stops:

    I think I love you.

I'm writing the essay on decorum that Mr. Jordan told me to do. When he said the word, I was pretty sure it meant respect. But I've got the dictionary down and am looking it up, just to be sure. I'm surprised. The definition does not include the word respect. This is what it says:

"decorum: (n); /di'kôrəm/

1. Keeping in good taste

2. Etiquette"

So like, keeping your clothes on in front of others would be an example of proper decorum. I get it. But I'm not one hundred percent sure what "etiquette" means. So I go ahead and look that one up. This is what it says:

"etiquette: (n); /ˈetikit/

The customary code of polite behavior"

I wasn't being polite then either.

I start thinking about examples of polite behavior. It makes me sad. Before Homecoming, I always thought I was a polite girl. I mean, I always say 'please' and 'thank you' even when it's just to other kids. I don't steal. I don't like to fight. I don't tell too many lies. I don't dress in Goth clothes. I don't like to do anything too crazy. I don't look like your typical "outcast."   But then… when I start thinking about what it means to be polite, I can't think of any specific time when I was polite to somebody else.

That makes me sad.

I start thinking about what it might be mean to be nice to someone, to always be polite. I write about it in the paper. About how I'm going to think before I act, how I'm going to do more things besides just saying 'please' and 'thank you.' I'm going to be helpful. I'm going to be the most polite kid you've ever seen. And I'm going to do it not because I got in such trouble but because people who are polite, they are the ones that get loved.

I mean, think about it.

At school, it's not outcasts that are loved.

It's the cheerleaders and the jocks. And they are loved not only because they play sports but also because they are nice to everybody. They are happy. It makes me wonder if anything bad ever happens to them at all. What would they do if they were given my life for even one day? I don't think they'd do too well.

Still, they are loved.

I am not.

So if I have to pretend to be happy, I think I can do it. If I have to be polite so that others will think I'm like them, then I will be polite. I think of the paper I wrote on Cinderella not long ago. I don't wish to go to a ball. My greatest wish is to be normal, is to be loved. Nick says he loves me. And maybe, just maybe, I know now how to keep him loving me.

***** ***** *****

My mom's going to see my dad again. I got out of having to go by telling her I really didn't feel good. I've got at least three hours to kill without her ever knowing I was out of the house at all. At first, I thought she was never going to let me stay here at the house. She thinks it's important that I go to see Dad. If only she knew how unimportant it is. Anyway, I finally convinced her I just didn't feel very good and needed to lay down. After she agreed to let me stay home by myself, she made me take some Tylenol for my non-existent fever and made sure I was in the bed.

I thought she was never going to leave. But she did!

Nick has family in town, staying at his house. And we're kind of getting bored of the park. So I told him he could hang here, at my house, for a few hours. Until Mom's due back anyway. I didn't use to lie to Mom. But she'd understand, I mean, she has to remember what it feels like to have someone like you and want to spend time with you. Or, actually, maybe she's forgotten and that's why she makes it so hard. What am I supposed to do? Stay by myself forever?

I told him to be here at noon. Its twelve thirty now. Maybe he's not coming. I'm getting worried about that. I mean, he'll have to be gone by three. Time is ticking. What if he's decided he doesn't love me anymore, and doesn't show up? Maybe I should text him, to make sure he's okay, and that he remembers what time...

The sound of the doorbell jerks me away from my phone. He's here! I pat my hair down in the mirror and race down the steps. Just to make sure it's not my mom come back for something she forgot, I peek out the window first. He's there. Standing there on my porch. My heart leaps into my throat as I open the door.

"Hey."

"Hey," he says.

I step away from the door, and he walks in.

"Your mom gone?" he asks. "I waited a little bit, just to make sure. My mom never leaves the house on time."

I smile. "Yeah. She's gone."

"Where'd she go?"

I shrug and lie. Again. "Um, I don't know. She said she'd be gone a couple hours, though. She told me she should be back by three."

"Cool. What do you have to drink?"

We walk into the kitchen and he sits at the small white dining table. I give him a Coke and we spend the next few minutes talking about nothing. It's weird how the air around you can make you feel cramped.

"So… what'cha want to do?" I ask, shrugging my shoulders. "I've got some movies or…"

"Hm, do you have a Playstation?"

I do. It's not mine; it's my dad's, actually. But he's in jail so we can play it. It doesn't take long until I start to relax, once we're playing the game. It's fun. And he's really good. When he wins, he shouts, "yes!" and I laugh. It's cute, how he likes to win a lot. It reminds me of a little boy.

"So…" I ask, looking over at him as he turns the PlayStation off. "What's this thing you got planned for me on Saturday?"

He doesn't look at me, kind of looks off to the side. He must be nervous. That's so sweet! Somebody's nervous over me!

"It's nothin' big," he mumbles.

"It's a present? Why can't you give it to me til Saturday?"

"It's not really a present, it's just… I can't get it til then."

I smile.

He looks away from me.

"I can't wait til to see what it is."

"I know. I really just want it to be a surprise, that's all. Is it ok if we just don't talk about it? It's hard to keep it a secret when you keep talking about it."

He sounds like he's getting a little mad. So I give in. "Okay. That's okay. I'll just try to wait."

He goes back to being sweet. He smiles at me and it makes everything okay for real. He reaches out a hand and touches my face. "You're so beautiful."

What am I supposed to say to that? The pretty cheerleaders would know. But I'm not a pretty cheerleader. Right now, I don't even care. My heart beats so fast I can almost hear it in my chest. I don't say anything, but I drop my eyes to my lap.

"I'm glad we didn't have to go to the park today," he says and scoots closer to me on the couch. The air in the room, it's like it shrinks. I forget to breathe for a minute because he's got this look in his eyes and it's so warm. Even when he's not saying anything at all right now, he's making me feel pretty and special and... wanted. Truly wanted.

"You are?" I ask. "Why?"

He shrugs and looks to the side for a minute. Then he reaches out and touches my face again. I feel his fingers go into my hair. "Well, I just... I've wanted to do something with you. You know how I told you about my dream? Where I'm kissing you?"

My mouth goes dry.

"I thought it's time to see what it would feel like for real."

I swallow hard. I should tell him no. I didn't mean for this to happen today. I mean, he might think he wants to kiss me but I know that he really doesn't. I hear Dad in my head, telling me that a real girl opens her mouth when she's kissed, that she gives it back too. In other words, I'm a sucky kisser. And there's that whole thing with me and kissing. Kissing is special. It's something I always thought I wouldn't do with just anybody.

But he did say he loves me.

And he's so cute.

I wonder...I wonder if it is different...

I don't know he's leaning toward me until I feel his mouth on mine. It feels different than Dad's.... Nick's is soft for one thing. Dad's was always real hard, rough. Nick's is not. I feel his tongue rubbing my lips. I don't know that I open my mouth until I feel his tongue in mine. I don't even notice the saliva, like I do with Dad. All I feel is warm. I sit frozen in spot, with his mouth on mine, until I feel him push his hands under my shirt. I jerk back, shaking my head, looking stunned.

His hand gets caught under my shirt, it rises up. Not much, but I know he sees the cuts because he frowns.

"What are those?" he asks. He grabs the edge of my shirt and pulls it up. I'm not warm anymore, I'm cold. This, the grabbing, I'm used to. I remember. I haven't forgotten. I start to freak out, and try to pull my shirt out of his hands, but then I realize it's too late. He's already seen. I let out a breath I didn't even know I was holding and stop fighting.

"Those are cuts." He says.

I shrug, tugging the edge of the shirt down. He grabs my arm, tugs the sleeve up. When he sees all the cuts, he curses. "You cut yourself?"

He makes it sound like I'm an alien from outer space, so it's easy to get mad at him. I shrug and stand up off the couch. I wish he wouldn't talk about the cuts. I wish he'd tell me what he thinks of the kiss. The longer he goes without saying anything about the kiss at all, the more I think he thinks it was awful.

"Why do you cut yourself?" He's got a funny look on his face. It's not concern. It doesn't look like worry. But he's not laughing either. It hits me that I don't know him well enough to know what he thinks. But I let him kiss me. That makes me feel weird inside. I don't know if he cares or not, but I want him to care. The mad goes away. I feel it draining out of me. I push my hair off my face and sit back down on the couch beside him.

I shrug. "I dunno. I've done it for awhile now."

"What do you cut yourself with?"

"A knife, what else? I mean, sometimes it's a razor. I've got both in my room." I hesitate; wait for a minute before looking at him in the face. "Do you think it's stupid?"

He shakes his head. "No. I think it's

cool. You know, brave like. I mean, I wouldn't want to cut myself. It's got to take guts to do that." His tone still doesn't quite match his words but I want to believe him. I want to believe him so bad. I've never been called brave before. Or cool. He called me cool.

I raise up my sleeve on my arm and show him where I carved stuff. The word "freak" is there. And a couple hearts too. Carved into my skin.

"Whoa," he says. Then, "You probably shouldn't do that, you know."

I shrug. "I like doing it."

"Why?"

"I don't know. Same reason you like to drink and look at pictures, I guess." I don't know why I snap that but he nods. Then he smiles at me. "Okay, good point." Then he says he has to go. But as he heads for the door, he turns and looks at me again. "Don't forget about Saturday. You can be there?"

Forget about Saturday? It's all I've been thinking about for a week. Nobody has ever wanted to give me such a big present that I had to wait a whole week for it.

"I won't forget," I promise. "I'll be there."

It's not until he's gone, when I go back to my room to lie on my bed and stare at my arms, that I start to think that maybe I shouldn't have shown him the carvings. I mean, I think of it as art. But most people probably don't. And it was a lot to take in at once, learning that I cut and then that I carve words and pictures into my skin. I start to worry that I shouldn't have told him. I grab my phone without thinking too much to text him. *"Hey, sorry about the whole cutting thing. Hope I didn't freak you out."* It takes a few minutes but then my phone beeps with a message back: *"It's cool, don't worry. See you Saturday, honey."*

I close my eyes and smile.

Maybe I'm not a cheerleader. But I am *Honey.*

***** ***** *****

The next day at school is just like the other days have been. People stare at me. They whisper when I walk past them. At lunch, I can see them looking at their phones and then up at me. I still hear the awful names being said as I walk past. Slut is a popular one. I don't know how just flashing a couple people is really a slut but then that doesn't surprise me. I haven't ever really understood the people my age. In fact, even though school is really pretty much the same, I just don't care.

I like English. I usually listen to Mrs. Simmons. But today, I don't hear a word she says. I just sit in the only left handed desk in the classroom, staring at my notebook. In the margins, I've written the word "honey" in block letters about half a dozen times. I've written the words "Nick + Taya" lots to, my favorite of which has my name in blue ink and his in red. Like love.

I started writing him a letter. I don't know when I'm going to give it to him. While Mrs. Simmons talks about propositions and sentence structure, I turn to the back of my notebook, where the letter I'm writing is. I re-read it, thinking about how Nick might feel when he reads it.

Dear Nick

I know we didn't really start out on the right foot. But I remember that awful night. I remember when I first saw you. I wondered what your name was, and thought you were so cute. When I had to kiss you that night, I was embarrassed. But it was also exciting. You're the first boy I've ever even thought about kissing. You're the first boy I've ever kissed for real.

Hanging out with you is so cool and awesome. You're very funny. And sweet. I love how you'll push me on the swings at the park. I'll never forget how you let me sit in your lap and you swung us both. I felt like I was flying. Every time with you is like that, though. Special.

I didn't know what love felt like before you. But I think this is it. I've wanted to say it for a long time now, ever since you did, but I was still a little embarrassed. But love needs to do something and doesn't care about being embarrassed. And I need to tell you this so much. It's all I can think about.

I love you."

I sign my name on it and fold it in half. Then I fold it again. I curl my hand around it and hold it tight. I don't have a class with Nick but sometimes I get lucky and see him in the hallways. We have to walk the same way to get to fourth period. So if I time it right, if I wait fifteen seconds to get up out of my seat after the bell rings and then walk at just the right pace, I can sometimes see him when I turn the corner. He usually don't talk to me in school but sometimes he'll smile. Once, he even winked at me. It is the only time in the school day that I can hope to get a glimpse of him. I've gotten pretty good at the timing but today I am nervous. Because today is important. I am going to give him the letter. That's what love is…. Putting your heart on your sleeve because you love him and know he loves you too.

The bell rings. In my head, I count to fifteen slowly before getting up. I walk at his pace---quick but not fast—out of the classroom. My heart starts beating faster when I get halfway down the hall. I hope I see him. There's a ton of kids in the hallways but I don't even see them. I don't hear anything either. My eyes are just focused on the end of the hallway.

We almost collide.

My heart stops a minute, then races. He smiles at me and nods. I hold out my hand and when he sees something in it, he grabs the letter. It's very quick. He keeps walking. He doesn't acknowledge I gave it to him at all. But he has it. I tell myself that that's all that's important.

Because that's what hope does.

It is three thirty in the morning.

Actually, to be more accurate, it is three thirty three in the morning. I've not been asleep yet. Yesterday was really bad at school. This jerk in gym offered to give me five dollars if I'd flash *him*, ten if I'd let him touch. They say time makes people forget stuff but it's been two weeks and nobody has forgotten yet. Plus, I messed up the timing somehow and missed the chance to see Nick yesterday in the hallway. Then, he had to do homework and couldn't get on instant messenger like usual. So I had to go all day without talking to him, or seeing him. I had to go all day by myself.

      I haven't had to cut in about a week. That's a long time for me. But seeing or talking to Nick helps. It's not that I've been trying not to cut... I just haven't wanted to. The kids at school still bother me. Sometimes I still get mad at them, especially when they say really stupid stuff like the guy yesterday. But now, most of the time, I don't care. I just pretend they don't exist. They are not the ones who are important, so they don't matter. I just come home, do my homework and then get on instant messenger and chat with Nick. That makes me forget everything and by the time we're done talking, I haven't even thought about the blade.

Today, though, I almost had to. Dad called and wanted to talk to me. He said he misses me and wants to make sure I come visit him next week. He says he's got something to tell me and Mom. I don't even care what he has to tell me and Mom. I don't want to go. He told me I'm getting real pretty and asked if any of the boys at school like me. I didn't tell him about Nick because, I mean, are you kidding me? I haven't even told Mom about Nick because she'll tell Dad. Talking to Dad makes me feel like a clumsy little girl. It makes me think bad things, things that I haven't thought of in awhile, and I get this little bubble of panic in my heart. It's like when you listen to really loud music. At first, it's okay, but then the longer you hear it, the bigger headache you get until finally the same music is driving you up the wall and it's either turn the music off or get out of the room.

Talking to Dad makes me feel like I'm trapped, like there's not enough room around me.

I tried texting Nick but he didn't answer right then. I tried going outside to the back yard and lying in the hammock. Nothing worked. The only thing that helped was cutting. Two little gashes, though, and that's it. Because I remembered that, when I woke up, it'll be Saturday. Today's the day that I am supposed to meet Nick. He's going to have the surprise for me.

That's why I haven't been able to sleep all night. I've been lying here, tossing and turning, since eleven. I've taken two baths so that I will be extra clean. I've painted my nails a pretty red color. I've got the outfit I'm going to wear out already; it's a white skirt with a blue V-neck top. It makes me look and feel grown-up.

To try and get some sleep, I think of Nick. I see him pushing me on the swings. I see him, with his beautiful eyes, smiling at me the day he surprised me by bringing us a picnic to the park. I think of when he put his hand on my face and how warm that felt. And I think of his kiss too. It's hard to be away from him. I feel like we never get to see each other because we don't have the same schedules at school and, this week, he's been hanging out with his guy friends more.

That's okay, I remind myself, *Today is the day that he's going to spend with you.* My eyes start to feel heavy and I roll over to my side, wrap my arms around my pillow and close them. I've got a few hours left to sleep and I need to make the most of them, so that I'm rested. Today is going to be a great day.

***** ******

The sun is shining brightly. It's almost November but the weather is still nice out. Brisk, but not cold. Windy, but not chilly. It's beautiful too. The leaves are brightly colored and falling from their branches. The wind swirls them up around my feet as they fall. It's a great day for a walk.

This morning, Nick texted and changed the meeting place. He said the meadow behind the school's football field is best. I'm not sure why, but I don't care. If he told me to walk to California, I'd make it happen. He sounds like an excited little boy when he talks to me about the surprise. It's like he can't wait to share it with me. But that's just the way he is, Nick. He's sweet all the time.

No games are taking place this weekend so the football field is deserted. Images of Homecoming flash in my head, but I push them away. None of that matters. I walk right on the field to take a short cut to the meadow. The meadow isn't really part of the school's property but it lies so close to the football field that it might as well be. The kids call it the meadow but it's really more like a field. The grass is so tall that it's like weed. Dandelions and sunflowers grow everywhere in it. Bumblebees and flies make their home here too.

I don't see Nick in the meadow. I see three other boys, though, as I get closer. It takes me a minute but then I see that one of them is Derrick. A bad feeling creeps up my stomach, churning it, but I walk on, scanning the meadow for Nick. All I see are trees and grass.

"Hey, Taya," Derrick calls.

I nod toward him, mumble hello, but stay far enough away from him and his friends that they don't think I'm interested in talking.

"What'cha doing here?" One of the other guys asks.

I shrug. "Nothin', just waiting on a friend."

The boys walk closer.

"Who?" Derrick asks.

I don't answer him. Nick doesn't want Derrick to know that he spends so much time with me.

"Hey," the tall, gangly, red-haired boy says, "Derrick, ain't this the girl whose took that cool picture?"

"Yeah, it sure is." Derrick says. By this time, they are close enough that I can see their eyes. Derrick steps in front of me, the red-haired boy steps behind me and the third guy, the one with black hair, steps to my side. I feel trapped. I look over their heads for any sight of Nick. He is always late. But, what if he's not coming?

I try to walk around Derrick but he sidesteps me, blocking my way.

"You know, my friend is a little late and I have to get back home. So I think I'll just text him later. I'm going to go on home now." My voice doesn't even wobble. I turn around and try to walk away but the red haired guy behind me stops me. He reaches out and his hand touches my chest.

I jerk backward. "What are you doing? Move." I try to make my voice sound as brave as Nick thinks I am. But it wobbles a little.

"We don't want to do nothing wrong, Taya, do we boys? We were just thinking, though, that maybe you could show us what you got again. You know, flash us a quick one." The black haired one says, reaching out and trying to grab the end of my shirt. I beat him to it, grab my shirt and step backwards. I run into Derrick. He grabs my arms while the red haired guy goes for my shirt.

"Raise it up, come on, man, get it up. Nick said she's got knife marks on her. I seen them in the picture, but I must have been really drunk at Homecoming, because I don't remember the cuts." Derrick says.

I hear Nick's name.... but it doesn't sink in. All that I understand is that they are going to take my clothes off. Dad flashes in my mind. I was just a little girl then. I never did anything. Nobody knows except me and him. I know what will happen if they take my clothes off. And the thought makes me go a little crazy. I do what I never did before: I scream.

I scream as loud as I can. They've got my arms so I can't move them, but I shake my head back and forth as hard as I can. I throw one of my legs back until I kick one of them. I hear one of them laughing, but I don't know which one of them it is. One of the guys I don't know says, "Man, he didn't tell us what a hellcat she is."

"Yeah," Derrick adds, squeezing my butt cheeks. "If he put up with this for two weeks, he deserves the fifty dollars."

I am kicking and screaming so hard we fall to the ground. I scramble to my knees but one of them gets my ankle and hauls me back. I fall on my face, my nose hits the ground, dirt fills my mouth. I feel the adrenaline rushing through my whole body but I know what will happen. Soon, it will fade and I won't have any energy left to fight. Angry tears fill my eyes.

I just can never win.

All of a sudden, nobody's touching me. One of them yells, "Nick! Man, somebody's comin', let's get out of here!" and I see another boy, Nick, run from behind a tree.

"Surprise, Taya!" he yells as they race away.

I am shaking. I don't have a shirt on, again, and I am crying. I lay there in the dirt until I hear a man's voice say, "Are you alright,

young lady? I heard you screaming and came a-
running.... Oh, Lord a mercy, what have them
boys done to you?" He leans down and scoops
me up into his arms. I know him. He is the
school janitor. He is a hero.

He takes me into the school, lets me put
my shirt he grabbed from the ground back on.
He gets me a Snicker's bar and a Coke from the
vending machine and tells me he'll call the
police. But I don't want him to. Telling doesn't
help anything. Besides, they didn't get to do
anything. They didn't really hurt me, not like
they were going to.

After I stop shaking, I ask him to take me
home. I am afraid of walking alone. Nick
knows the route I take and they might be waiting
for me. I am scared but I don't tell the janitor
that because, if I do, he'll call the police. If he
calls the police, they'll call Mom. So I just ask
him to take me home.

My lip is swollen. I bit it real hard when
that punk pulled me backward, making my face
hit the ground. I am dirty everywhere. I can
still feel their hands grabbing for my shirt. And
I can still here Nick's voice yelling "surprise!"

I just want to disappear.

I just want to disappear.

I just want to die.

When I was four years old, my

mother took me to a park for the Fourth of July
fireworks display. The park was full of people.
It wasn't very crowded, but no one had lots of
space around them either. I remember the loud
music blaring from speakers. Everyone was
happy. Kids were playing with hula hoops,
families were throwing ball. Right in front of
where we'd sat down our blanket and picnic
basket was an Amish family. The mother wore a
black dress. I remember that, because I
remember thinking about how hot she probably
was. There were five kids with the family. I
remember watching them and wishing I could
play with some of the girls. They had such fun
toys. They had a Frisbee. And the smallest
child, a little boy, had a bottle of bubbles. He
went around us laughing while he blew bubbles.

Vendors pushed their carts around, trying to get everybody to buy something. There were carts that sold hot dogs and nachos. There were carts that sold snow-cones. And there were carts that sold toys too. One of them sold a multi-colored wand that lit up. When it was turned on, the lights raced up and down the wand. It looked like a wand a princess really should have. I tried to get my mother to look, but she was too busy talking to another mom to pay attention to me pulling on her arm.

I didn't know any better, I didn't know then that I had to have money for the toy. So I followed the cart, thinking that Mom was right behind me. I tried to catch up with it, but it swerved and it seemed like a swarm of people covered it up. I couldn't see it anymore. When I turned around to go back to my Mom, I couldn't see my Mom either. I didn't see our blanket. I didn't see hear my mom talking. And I had no idea which way to go to find her.

I was scared, and I started crying.

I started walking, trying to find her, but then I remembered her telling me that if I ever couldn't find her, to stay still. That she would come to me. She told me not to wander further away, but to stop and wait for her to come. It was hard. I thought I should walk, but I didn't know where to walk to.

I sat down on the grass and waited

A lady I did not know asked me if I was okay. She asked me if I knew where my mom was. I told her no. She told me to come with her, but I said no. I told her that Mom told me to wait for her. To stay still and not move. The lady nodded and said that was a good rule. And she waited with me. She sat down and talked to me. She kept me from crying. But I was still scared. I was only four years old but I remember being scared that maybe Mom wouldn't come to me. Maybe she wouldn't find me. What if she didn't even try?

It didn't take long until I saw Mom running through the crowd. She was crying. When she saw me, she grabbed me in her arms and hugged me tight. I remember the smell of her lilac perfume and how good it felt to be safe in her arms. Waiting for her was probably the bravest thing I had ever done in my whole life.

Until today.

I woke up a minute ago in the bed with my eyes swollen from crying and five new cuts on my arms. I made a real deep one on the inside of my elbow. It took it a long time to stop bleeding. I carved the word "stupid" on my left wrist. I hold both my arms above my head and look at the scars. The words "stupid" and "freak" are carved on them. Stupid freak. That's what I am.

I believed him.

I believed Nick when he told me I was beautiful. I believed him when he told me I was cool. I believed him when he told me I was a friend. I believed him when he said he loved me.

I was stupid.

I was a freak.

I have to go back to school today.

He will be there.

They all will.

I could skip today; tell my mom I am sick. But that janitor, he said he'd check up on me today, see how I was doing. I told him I was fine. I begged him not to tell anyone, and he said he wouldn't, but if he looks for me and finds I'm not at school, he might. He might go to Mr. Jordan. And if he does that, my mom will find out.

I have to go.

I roll out of the bed; pull my black sweater out of the closet and a pair of jeans. I brush my hair and pull it over my shoulders to help hide my face. I don't want Mom to think something's wrong with my face. Half an hour later, I am staring at the school from the window of the Mom's car.

I haven't noticed before how big this place is. It's huge. And yet it feels so small right now. It's getting hard to breathe, just looking at it. I sit still for a minute. They are in there. Derrick. The other two boys. Nick. What if they try to get me alone somewhere? Mom drops me off at school, but I walk home. What if they wait for me this afternoon after school to finish what they started?

"You awake, kiddo? Time to go." Mom's voice sounds happy and light. But I'm not supposed to go. She's supposed to take one look at my face and know something's not right. She's supposed to ask me what's wrong, tell me she'll take care of it. I'm supposed to just wait for her. Only this time, she doesn't know I'm lost.

I blow a breath out my mouth and open the car door. I can't believe how brave I am. I mumble goodbye and walk slowly into the school. Kids swarm over me. The noise level is high. I don't see anybody at all. I make it to my homeroom class and sit with my head down.

Nobody acts different than they have been. I don't hear any new whispers. Nobody cares that I'm even here. Which is good. It means the boys haven't started any more lies. Maybe no one will ever have to know.

My stomach hurts. It hurts real bad. When the bell rings, I go to the bathroom. I stay in the bathroom, skipping first period so that I can sit on the toilet without anybody looking at me for a whole fifty minutes. I go to second period, though. And that's when I notice that the whispers are back. Somebody says, "Hey, Taya, you wanna try me?"

I bite my lip hard and ignore it. I ignore everything. I just slide down in my seat and pretend they don't exist. Only pretending doesn't really help when you can hear them right beside you. They know you can hear, but they still keep talking. That's what high school bullies do. They don't really knock you down to the ground every day. Instead, they make others think you're something you're not. Sometimes, the good bullies, they do it so well that they make you think it too.

By the time Mrs. Simmon's class rolls around, I'm done being sad and embarrassed. Now, I'm just plain mad. I want to know what they are saying. I want to know what exactly Nick did. I want to see him tell me he lied to me. I want him to say it to my face. My stomach starts hurting again, and feels really nauseous as the clock edges towards the end of English. When the bell rings, I count slowly to fifteen, and then leave the classroom, walking at just the right speed.

I round the corner just as he does. We almost bump into each other. Gathering up all my bravery, I say, "Nick."

He shrugs and starts to walk away but I grab his arm. "If you don't talk to me," I threaten, "I will start saying the truth. And I will make a huge scene. I will tell them how you pushed me on the swings. I will tell them how you said I was beautiful. I will yell it out in the hallway."

He laughs and shrugs a shoulder. "They already know, Taya."

I frown. "They know what? That you told me I was beautiful?"

"Yeah. They even know I told you I loved you."

I frown. That doesn't make any sense. A small bubble of hope pierces through the icy cold wall in my heart. Maybe I had it wrong. Maybe he just happened to be there at the same time. Maybe…

"How do they know?"

"You're such a kid. They know because I told them. It was a joke, you know? Me, going out with you. We made a bet that I could get you to give me more than a flash in one month." He shrugged. "It was a bet, that's all. I don't really want to hang out with you. And how could I really love somebody that does something so stupid to her body? So yeah, go ahead. Tell them. They've already seen pictures of your messed up body."

Water is swirling around my brain. I feel very light headed. My face flushes with heat. I think I might pass out. I bend my head.

"What about Saturday?" I ask.

"They wasn't really going to do nothing. You know that. They just wanted to scare you some. Make you think I was the saving hero. But then I was just going to walk away." He laughed. "I did walk away, didn't I?"

My mouth goes dry.

Without answering him, I move to the side and start walking. I don't really see anything in front of me. I accidentally knock a kid in the shoulder because I don't really see anyone. I'm just walking, like on auto pilot.

I've been a bet.

I've been a joke.

I was never a friend.

I was never beautiful.

I was never loved.

I'm just a freak.

A stupid freak.

I skip the rest of classes. I don't want anyone to call my mom, tell her I wasn't there, so I go into the bathroom again and hide in the stall. I don't cry. When the bell rings and the bathroom is empty, I lie down on the floor in the stall, curl my legs up to my chest and pray to die.

You know...

Nobody ever tells you this, but you can feel your heart break. It feels like the air in the room is being sucked out and you can't breathe. It feels like something deep inside your chest is cracking. It feels like a cut. A deep, deep cut. It stings at first, then burns a path along the broken edges. And it leaves you with the very sure knowledge that it will never be whole again.

***** *****

I skip the next three days of school. It takes that long for me to get over it. It takes that long for me to be able to drag in a full breath of air. I am going back tomorrow. I've practiced. I've stood in front of my bedroom mirror and said out loud the things that they are going to say about me. That way, I've already heard it, so it can't hurt me.

I'm taking two small razor blades with me. I've hidden them in my bra. It makes me feel safe. If anybody thinks I'm just a joke anymore, if anybody lays even a finger on my skin without me telling them to, I will carve into their skin.

I'm done being nice.

I'm done being quiet and just taking it. I'm done doing nothing about nothing. If they want to talk about me, fine. I'll give them something to talk about. Playing it safe never got me nothing.

I turn the hair dryer off and turn around. I don't look up until I put the hairdryer down on the sink. Then I raise my eyes and look in the mirror for the first time at my new, purple hair.

Purple hair is against the rules at school. I won't get away with having it for long. That's okay. I just need it for one day. I just need it long enough that the kids in even just homeroom can see it and start that gossip chain flowing. I'm going to raise my chin and stare them straight in the eye too. I'm going to dare them to tell. Then, when I get in trouble for it, I'll dye it back. But I'll be the winner because they'll be talking about something different than the time I was somebody's bet.

I am a big deal in school today. Not one person has said a word about how many days I've missed. Not one person has said a word about Nick or Derrick or any of them. Nobody has said anything to me at all. They just stare at my hair and whisper. It's all so stupid. It's purple hair, big deal.

But it is a big deal.

I got called down into the principal's office for it. He told me I would have to go home and I cannot come back to school until I have a "traditional" color on my head. He said it gives people the wrong impression. He said he knows I'm a smart kid. I've always had really good grades. So why would I want everybody to think I'm a punk kid?

Because being a punk kid is better than being called a slut.

Mom gets to the school and doesn't say a word on the drive home. She is speechless. I don't think she knows what to say to me. She drops me off at the house and tells me not to go anywhere. Then she drives off again.

I'm not upset.

I knew I would never get away with having purple hair for long. So it's okay that Mom's probably going to the store to buy some ugly, normal color for me. That's not the point. The point is, everybody saw me. The point is, I took control of what they talk about.

So I win.

Mom comes back with the ugliest shade of brown I have ever seen in my life. I tell her it is ugly. She says, "sorry. You should have thought about that before you died it purple." So that I don't have to deal with her being mad at me, I dye my hair the ugly brown color.

When I get out of the shower, I stare at myself again. I look more like me now that my hair is not purple. I look almost normal. At least, my face and my hair do. You can't see the rest of me because of my clothes.

That's another thing.

I don't like any of my clothes anymore.

They are too bright, too clean, too… pretty. Why should I wear pretty things if the body I'm in isn't pretty? The body doesn't matter, it doesn't matter what you do to it. It's just skin. What I wear is another thing that I can control. School rules say I can't have holes in my clothes. But I can make them *look* torn. I rake scissors down a pair of my jeans until they are nearly torn. I put my black jeans in with Mom's whites. They come out bleached weird. I think they are cool. It's more like me.

Mom told me I don't have many clothes anymore. She gave me money to go shopping for some and took me to the mall. We ended up fighting because I just wanted to buy black clothes. There was a black shirt that had a skull on it. I wanted it but Mom said no. Used to, I would have just said 'okay.' I never would have argued with her. But I did. I told her I should be able to buy whatever I wanted. I'm the one wearing it, so I should be able to choose what it is. I don't know if she thought what I said had merit or if she was just so surprised to hear me argue with her... whatever the case was, she bought me the shirt but told me I could not wear it to school. She called it a 'compromise.' I didn't wear it to school.... Not really. The next day, I wore a normal shirt to school but then, when I got there, I pulled the skull shirt out of my backpack and put it on in the bathroom.

My clothes. My choice.

I'm wearing it today. I'm sitting with it on in the back of Mrs. Simmons' class. I'm usually real good in English. We have a test today, a big one, over the Scarlett Letter. I didn't read the book. I would have but I just didn't care. I didn't see the point in reading a book. I had other things to do, like cut. It don't matter, though. I'm an Ace in English; I can pass any test in this subject anytime. I can pass a test in most subjects without ever studying. It's a gift I have. It's one of the only gifts I have. I'm not really worried about the test... until she gives it to me.

I read the first question and blink. It seems like a simple question. It doesn't sound like a trick one. It's just asking the name of the two main characters. I should be able to know that. But I don't. So I skip it and go to the next question. I don't know the answer to it either. I guess at some of the questions, trying to make my answers sound smart, and I leave some of the blanks empty because I don't even know what to guess. It's the first time I've ever wished that the English test had been over grammar instead of a book. That's how bad it is.

Failing a test makes you feel dumb. And I definitely failed that test just now. There's no way I got even half of those questions right. I look around the class at my classmates. They probably got most of it right. I see Dee. Dee is part of a gang. I know she is, everybody knows she is. A Goth gang. She wears only black; she puts really black eye make-up on and then uses blood red lipstick. She wears her black hair straight down over her eyes. She does drugs too. Everybody knows that.

I look away from her and back down at my own clothes. My skull t-shirt, my bleached jeans. How did I turn into Dee? It's as if the bubble in my heart pops. Tears sting my eyes for no reason. It's just a test I failed. But it's the third test this week. I look like a Goth gangster. I had purple hair. All of a sudden, it just feels stupid.

When the bell rings, I don't go to my next class. Instead, I walk downstairs and right out the front door of the building. No one stops me. They will probably call my mom later, when they realize I'm not in any more classes today. But I don't care. School used to make me feel smart. Now, it just makes me feel stupid. It doesn't matter how hard I try to convince myself that I don't care what the other kids think or say... the truth is, I do care.

Because they're right.

I *am* a freak. I can wear different clothes. I can argue with my mom. But it doesn't change the truth. I will never be anything different than what I already am. I will never be anything at all.

***** ******

Mom's still at work when I get home. She got a job as a secretary when Dad got arrested. She don't get home until about five thirty, sometimes six. I've been eating a lot of beanie weenies and cereal since she doesn't feel like cooking when she gets home. She tried, when she first started the job, to keep cooking dinner every night. But then, I felt bad for her because I knew she was tired, so I told her I wasn't hungry. She didn't make dinner and then, before long, it was just a thing. That she didn't make dinner anymore. But it's not a big deal, I mean it's not that I need her to or anything. I just remember eating together before. You don't know all the things you'd miss until you don't have it anymore.

I'm used to it now though. I better be. Dad went in front of the same judge he'd seen before. The judge got mad that he was back and sentenced him to a really long time. He probably won't be able to sweet talk his way out of this one. I didn't say anything when he was arrested. I didn't cry. I just stood there and watched. I think he knows, though. When the cops were putting the handcuffs on him, he looked up and caught my eye. He stared at me like there was this big secret between us. There was more than one secret. I think he knows I called the cops. Or maybe not. Maybe it's just that a little part of me hopes he knows. Most of me hopes he *doesn't* know because he would be furious. But a small little part hopes he knows that he screwed over the wrong person one too many times.

Mom borrowed my "blue-eyed girl" shirt. I want to wear it to go walking. I like how it's loose and doesn't cling to my body. I go to the washer and dryer and look in the hamper for it, but it's not there. She must not have washed it yet. I go upstairs and into Mom's room. Her bed is not made yet; a shirt is thrown on the edge of it. The rest of the room, though, is spotless. I don't know how she keeps her room so clean.

I go into her closet and look around. I don't see it. Maybe she put it in her dresser. I open the bottom drawer, but there's nothing in there but underwear and socks. I close it and pull open the middle one. This one just has bras. I close it and pull open the top drawer. This one has three stacks of folded shirts. I start going through the first stack, then move on to the middle one. I reach my hand under the shirts to take them out, since that would be faster, and my fingers feel something cold and hard. I move the stack of shirts and then drop them on the floor.

A gun.

There is *a gun* in my mom's dresser.

I don't even know what to think about that. My mother is the safest person I know. Before this very minute, I would never have thought she would even let my dad bring a gun into the house. I try to think about why that gun may be here. It could have been my dad's. But that doesn't make any sense. If it was my dad's, Mom would have gotten rid of it after he was

arrested. She definitely wouldn't keep it around
in her shirt drawer. At least the Mom I know
wouldn't.

I stare at it. It's lying in the drawer. I
wonder if it's loaded. I look up toward the
bedroom door, then turn around to stare at the
clock sitting on Mom's bedside. She won't be
home for another hour or so. I look back at the
gun. This belongs to the woman who almost
didn't let me buy a shirt with a skull on it? That
can't be true, it would be too hypocritical.

And yet…

It's there. I see it.

I don't touch it. I grab the shirts and fold
them again, so it doesn't look like they were
touched, then I put them back in the drawer. I
close it and I walk out of the bedroom. I don't
even remember why I went in there. I don't
want to go for a walk anymore either.

There is a gun in this house.

There is a gun in my mom's drawer.

Why?

The question keeps running through my
head, again and again. I can see Dad owning a
gun. But he probably would have hidden it from
Mom. The only thing that makes sense is that
that's what happened---and then she found it
after he was arrested. I would believe that
except that the gun is in my mom's drawer.
Maybe she didn't want me to find it, and she

didn't know how to get rid of it. Dad probably would freak out if she sold it.

Still...

I can't seem to think about anything else for the next hour. Mom comes home, and I'm still thinking about it. I stare at her, watch her walk into the kitchen and fix a sandwich. She asks me about my day, I tell her it was fine. I want to ask her about the gun... but I don't know how. All I can think about is that I don't really know her. I thought I did. I thought I knew her really well. But the mom that made my school lunches every day until this year and who wanted Dad to go with me to the Father Daughter Dance would not keep a gun in her house. I wish I had held it. I wish I knew whether or not it was loaded.

Maybe she's scared. But, of what?

Maybe she's scared of Dad.

That makes a chill run down my spine. I sit up straighter at the kitchen table. My eyes narrow as she opens a Coke from the fridge and comes to sit down at the table beside me. I put my chin in my hand and watch her as if I've never seen her before.

Could she have been afraid of Dad too? Maybe the gun *is* hers. Maybe she got it in case he went too far one night, threatened her somehow. Memories race through my head. He ran a car over her foot once. He's hit her, sat on top of her on the floor and pulled her by the hair.

He's thrown her across a room. I've seen him do these things. I never thought he'd truly hurt her... but maybe Mom did.

I've lived with her for fifteen years and I never thought she was capable of owning or even touching a gun. I watch her as she moves around the kitchen, answer her questions about my day in a monotone, unable to think about more than the gun in the drawer upstairs. I don't eat anything, but I watch her until she's finished. I watch her until she says she's going to go shower and walks out of the kitchen.

My mom has a gun.

***** ***** *****

I came to school today.

I don't know why but I did. I'm dressed normal, too. No skull shirt stuffed in my backpack. No purple hair. Just a ponytail, red t-shirt and a clean pair of jeans. I'm just me. And that's why everyone is back to making fun of me. They whisper when I walk into the bathroom. They snicker mean words as I walk past them. Today, in Algebra II, this kid threw a wadded up piece of paper at me. When I picked it up, it said that word again: "Slut."

I don't even know his name.

It doesn't matter I've never been with anybody just because I wanted to be. It doesn't matter I never did anything with Nick. It doesn't matter that I didn't go to the field to screw anybody. It doesn't matter that the very thought of kissing somebody makes me break out in hives. It doesn't matter because I did that one stupid thing at the game. And that's all anybody remembers. Because that's the way it is and will always be: they only remember what they want to and only the interesting stuff. It doesn't matter if it's true or not. What matters is that they think it is. And because they think it is, I will never have any friends. I will never have a boyfriend. Dad's in jail, Mom's got a job, we have no reason anymore to leave this place. Even if we did, it wouldn't matter. I'd still do something stupid in the new place. Because that's what I am. Stupid.

The bell rings.

I stand up to go to Mrs. Simmons' class. I sit in the only left-handed chair watching Mrs. Simmons. I don't hear anything she says. But I watch her. She's been a very good teacher. She's the one that gave me the assignment on fairytales. My Cinderella had a happy ending. She told me I was smart and once she wrote "brilliant!" on one of my essays. She's been a good teacher.

By lunch time, I am just really tired. I go through the line, get a pizza stick and milk. I start to walk away but then decide to get a fruit cup too. I turn around to get one and bump into Ashlee, a cheerleader, one of the most popular girls in school. I bump her so hard she drops her tray. My face turns red with embarrassment as I watch her food spill all over the floor. Milk splashes on her cheerleading outfit and then the floor. She screams. Her friends instantly are around her, trying to help. I stand frozen in my spot.

"I—"

She looks up at me for the first time, her face red. "Can't you even just watch where you're going? Oh my God, Taya, just go away. You're just a waste of space."

My face turns red now and I'm horrified to find tears stinging the backs of my eyes. I turn around and walk away. I can feel everybody looking at me. I should help. But she told me to go away.

A waste of space.

Ashlee said it best: that's exactly what I am. A waste of space. I can't even walk without making something go wrong. I don't eat lunch. I throw it in the trash without ever sitting down. There's no way I can sit in this cafeteria and I'm definitely not hungry. The problem is that I just don't belong here.

My knees are wobbly. I can't walk home. But I can't stay where everybody can see me either. I walk down the halls of the school until

I turn a corner and find myself in the band room.
It is empty. There is a stage. I walk around the
side of the stage and find a small little hole that's
hidden. I crawl into the space under the stage.
It's tight. I have to lie on my side to fit. But
that's okay. It's better than anywhere else.
Here, no one will notice me.

    You're just a waste of space.

    No one will notice me here. I won't be
anybody's way here. I won't be taking up much
space here. I won't be a problem here. I keep
my eyes open and stare out. From here, I can
see the legs of the desks. In a few minutes,
when the bell rings and kids file in, I'll be able
to see their legs.

    Soon, music fills the room. Clarinets,
trumpets, violins. It sounds so pretty. I listen to
it without thinking about anything. I listen to it
until tears fill my eyes. I'm just taking up space,
space that's wasted by me. I don't know where
it comes from but I see a picture of the gun in
Mom's drawer. It's got a black handle. It's
perfect steel. I wonder if it's loaded. Just as
quickly as it comes, the picture of the gun is
gone. I just hear the music again. I listen to it
until the bell rings, and then I hear the kids file
out. Seven minutes later, more kids come in.
Music fills the room again. Fifty minutes later,
they leave. But I don't move. I don't want to
bump into anyone again. I don't want to waste
any more space.

My first bike was pink. It was a classic fifteen inch bicycle. Mom insisted I wear a helmet. It matched the bicycle, pink white polka dots all over it. I never rode with training wheels. One day, Dad just bought home this bicycle. He said he could teach me how to do it in no time. Mom was nervous. I remember that because she came outside and sat on the front porch to watch. She kept telling me to be careful and she asked Dad if I should have knee pads. He said, "I never had knee pads. She'll be fine."

I was so excited. I was scared, a little, but I was too excited to care about being scared. I jumped on the bike and was sure I could ride it without even having to learn how. I wobbled and fell. Dad didn't catch me. He let me fall. I hit the concrete. My knee and my elbow started bleeding and both were scratched real bad. Dad told me to get back up, that falling was part of riding a bike.

I didn't want to get back on.

Mom was furious. She ran to the road and picked me up, yelling at my dad. Dad told her to put me down, that if I didn't learn how to fall, then I would never learn how to do anything good. He told Mom to let me ride. I begged her not to make me go back outside.

Mom told Dad to get the hell away from me, that if that was his idea of teaching me something, then he would never teach me anything at all ever again. Mom took me inside and washed the blood away. She bandaged up the scrapes with a Mickey Mouse Band-Aid. She told me that she was sorry I'd fallen and that not to worry, I wouldn't have to ride if I didn't want to.

I was only six years old, but that day taught me something very important. I didn't learn anything important about handling disappointments. I didn't learn anything important about not quitting. I learned something that was bigger, something that I never forgot.

I learned Dad would let me fall.

It was another two years before I'd get back on a bike. When I did, I had knee pads, elbow pads and Mom at my side. She promised she wouldn't let me fall. And she didn't. She held the back of the seat and one of the handlebars. She told me that it would be wobbly and she told me how to pedal fast so that I could get some balance. She ran alongside the bicycle with me until I outdistanced her, until I was ready to go on my own. Then she stood back and cheered me on.

I was proud of myself. I loved the freedom that rushed over me as the wind blew my hair and the world flew by. I was on my bicycle all day after that. But every time I saw a bicycle, every time I went to get on mine, there was always a split second when I saw Dad's image standing back as I fell to the ground. Maybe that's because when someone fails to help you, when your own dad won't keep you from getting hurt, it proves to you that you're not worthy. That something must be wrong with you.

I've spent every year since looking for something to prove him wrong. I used to be good at school. I've made Honor Roll and Principal's List a couple times and once, I was even chosen as the Student of the Month for my whole school. But being good *at* something doesn't make you a good person. I was a good student. Big deal. I never got in trouble. I was really good at obeying. Big deal. The only thing that proves is that I'm good at school. It doesn't mean I'm a good kid. It doesn't mean that I'm a good friend. It doesn't prove that I'm a good daughter. It doesn't prove anything important.

All my life people have said what a good girl I am. All my life people have called me special. But every time they do, every time they would say something good about me, it would always feel like they were talking to someone else. Even today, when Mrs. Simmons tells me what a good job I did on an essay, there's always that second where I wonder if she's remembering who she's talking to. Does she really mean me, Taya, or does she have me confused with another student?

I've been thinking about my bike a lot.

I came to the park today. The one Nick and I used to meet up at. I bet he doesn't even remember that. He never comes here anymore, now that I'm not a bet he's out to win money off of. But I do. I still come here. There's this little girl riding her bike. She doesn't have training wheels either. She's about six years old, the same age I was when Dad let me fall. I've been sitting on this swing watching her ride around in circles for the last half hour. Her mom sits on the bench, playing on her phone. Every once in awhile, the little girl will call to her mom to watch her and the mother will lift her eyes from the phone, smile and wave. The little girl goes back to riding around by herself.

The mother gets off the phone and stands from the bench. She starts to chase the little girl, tells her she's going to get her. The little girl squeals with delight and pushes her feet faster and faster. I feel frozen in my spot. They don't see me, even though I'm right there in front of them. Nobody ever sees me.

After a few minutes, the mom stops running, pretends she's been beat. The girl gets off her bike and they lay down on the grass not far from me. The little girl lies down on her mom's stomach and they both stare up at the clouds. I can't hear what they are saying but I watch as the little girl points up at the sky. The mom does too. Then they both laugh.

Cloud shapes.

They are making shapes out of the clouds. I never played that game with anybody.

I tip my head back now and look up at the puffy white clouds. They just look like clouds to me. I don't see any shapes in them. I look for something; I look at one puffy cotton ball and try really hard to see something in its oval shape. But I can't see anything. All I see is a white oval.

It makes me very sad.

I know I'm different. I know I'm weird. A freak. But, once upon a time, I was born. I had to have been that little girl once. I had to have been able to look up at the clouds and see shapes in them.

Right?

It's scary to think that the answer is no. What if I was a mistake, a fluke on God's part? When Mom made us go to church every Sunday, my teachers always told us that everybody has a purpose. They told us that everybody was special and that everyone had a reason for being alive. But what if she was wrong? What if sometimes people just screw each other and mistakes happen?

I would be one of the mistakes.

I mean…. What else am I supposed to think? I can't even make shapes out of clouds.

I get up off the swing and they don't even turn their heads toward me as I walk by. It's like I'm invisible.

Even though people talk about me at school, I feel invisible. I feel that way a lot. I have my whole life. When I was good and teachers said I was smart, I thought they were talking about someone else. It didn't feel like they meant me. When people are mean to me, say bad things to me, it hurts because they see the real me. It hurts too much to listen to their words so I block it. I block everything they say until I just don't feel anything anymore. Cutting helps with that.

Or, at least, it used to.

Here lately, I have to cut deeper. And longer for it to help. Sometimes it's even hard to feel enough energy to cut. Last night, I just laid in the bed. I thought about getting the blade. I wanted to get the blade. But I didn't want to get up to go get it. I was just too tired. So I just laid there instead. I'm not really good enough to cut.

Cutting makes it feel better.

I shouldn't feel better. I should have to live with it, the knowledge that I'm just a nobody. I will never be like that little girl. I don't think I ever was that little girl. If I had of been like her, then my dad wouldn't have let me fall off my bike. He wouldn't have wanted to see me get hurt. He wouldn't have hurt me.

Once, when I was eleven, he told me he was just trying to teach me. He said he was trying to teach me how to be a good woman. He said boys would want someone who knew what they were doing. Because I needed to know how to be a good woman. Because I wasn't good.

I am glad Mom is still at work when I get home. I only have a few minutes before she'll get back. She could walk in anytime. But I have to know. I race up the stairs, going as fast as I can. I run into her room and jerk open the first drawer. I reach under the middle stack of shirts and pull it out.

It is heavy.

I want to hold it. I want to look at it for a long time, get to know everything about it. But I can't because she'll be home soon. I just have to know something. I look but I can't figure out how to open it up to see if there are bullets in it. It's got a chamber on it, the kind that rolls. But I don't know what that means. I don't know how to get the chamber to roll and I'm a little nervous. If it is loaded…

I have to look it up. I can do that. I can look it up. I put the gun back in the drawer, a little sad that I still don't know if it's loaded or not, and then fix the clothes. I am walking out of my mom's room when the front door opens.

She's home.

***** ***** *****

Two hours on the Internet can teach you a lot. My bedroom door is locked. And I have watched a handful of videos on guns. I think the gun in the drawer is a Smith and Weston. At least, it looks like the same kind. And I think I know how to check the chamber.

I practice, pretending the air is a gun. I watch the best video I can find about five times. There's a weird feeling in my stomach. It's not fear. It's not pain. I don't know how to describe the knot that it is. It feels like something big.

I have to wait.

I wait until Mom is in the shower. When I hear the water come on, I quickly walk into her room. I open the drawer, pull the gun out, press the release and then use my finger to push the chamber. I spin it and a feeling of power rushes over me. Chills run down my spine. The gun is not loaded. Not a single bullet.

I put it back under the clothes, shut the drawer and leave before the water turns off in the bathroom. A gun with no bullets isn't a gun. My stomach drops a little. It's like I'm being pulled by a magnet. I want to go back, make sure. The videos on the Internet were right, it was easy to handle. It was easy to check. But I was in a hurry; I might have missed seeing the bullet. I have never seen one. Maybe I overlooked it.

I can't go back now. Mom will be out of the shower soon.

I lay on my bed, staring at the ceiling.

I'm quiet but I feel restless.

I grab my headphones and turn music on. I jam to Pink but my mind is somewhere else. I swing my legs off the bed and walk over to my desk. I pull out a pen and some paper. I look around the room. What do I have? I don't really have much. After about five minutes of writing, my list is still short:

> Rocks
> CDs and IPod
> Clothes
> Pearl necklace

I don't cry until I list the necklace.

I got it when I was ten years old.

It wasn't really mine. It was my grandmother's. And it had belonged to my grandmother's mother. And my mother. I wasn't supposed to get it until I got married but, when I was ten years old, we had a dog. She was a beautiful, huge golden retriever. She had the most perfect color coat. And she loved everybody. She came up my ten year old waist. She was the friendliest dog you'd ever meet. She never jumped on anybody but she would lick you. When we first got her, she would come into my room and lay down at the foot of my bed. She would sleep there until morning. If Dad came in the room, she wouldn't leave. She'd just lay there. When he would leave, she'd come and lay down beside me. I would take my arms and wrap them around her big, furry self. Even today, I can smell her dog breath and feel the panting of her heart if I try hard enough.

Maxie had been with us two years. I know that for sure because, the day we got her, I wrote down her birthday in my diary and every year, we'd throw her a birthday party. She'd get all the doggie snacks she wanted and I didn't make her catch a ball for them. I loved that dog.

Late one night, we had to leave.

It was real important, the cops, they were real close. Dad thought they might show up at the house that very night. I was pulled out of bed and put in the car. I screamed for Maxie. But Mom said we couldn't take her. She promised that the cops would give her to a good family. She said that's what they did for animals left behind. I begged. I screamed. It was the worst fit I ever threw. But they both there wasn't room in the car and we were going a long, long way away. All the way across country. We didn't have time to stop every few hours for a dog. We didn't have the room in the car such a big dog like Maxie would need. We didn't have the money to buy the food Maxie would need. It was better for Maxie to stay behind.

You can feel your heart break.

I felt mine that night. I sat on my knees in the backseat of the car, looking out the rear windshield, with my hand pressed against the glass, until I couldn't see our neighborhood anymore. Then I lay down on the seat and cried myself to sleep.

Who was going to be there when Dad came to my room? Who was going to let me hug her furry hide? Who would play with me and who would feed Maxie snacks on her birthday? Who would know that her birthday was May 16? It was one of the loneliest and saddest times I can remember.

Dad never said a word about it.

But Mom...

Mom felt bad.

I think she must have missed Maxie too. One morning, when we got to the new house, I woke up to find the pearl necklace lying on the dresser. I knew what it was. I had asked her to wear it before, but she'd always said no. She said that it wasn't just a necklace, it was an heirloom. I loved the sound of that word. I used to say it to myself over and over. *Heirloom.* Being given an heirloom meant that you were old enough, and mature enough, to take care of it properly. It meant that you understood how special something was and would protect it. I used to listen to her tell me stories of when she got the necklace and how her mother got the necklace.

That necklace was a big deal.

And when I saw it lying on my dresser, I was excited for the first time since leaving Maxie. I was happy for the first time since we'd left my dog. I picked up gingerly, as if it might fall apart, and walked downstairs with it. I felt like a princess when I asked Mom if it was really mine now.

"Yes, honey, you can have it now. I think you're ready."

I beamed with pride when she took the necklace from me and put it around my neck to fasten it. I swore I was never going to take it off.

Of course, I did.
I had to.

But I've never forgotten that heirloom. I've never forgotten how special it is. Or what it means to Mom and to our family. I didn't have Maxie anymore but, sometimes, when the nights got really bad, when I was hurting very much, I would pull the necklace out after that and sleep with it tangled in my hand. I pretended that each of the pearls was a girl from our family and they were holding my hand. Maybe it sounds stupid. But it helped.

The idea of it not being mine anymore really hurts.

But I don't really deserve it. And it's not as if I would need it.

I get it out now and then I start making a list of the nice people in my life. That list is even shorter than the list of things I have.

Mama

Mrs. Simmons

That's two people.
I had four things on my list.
All I can think of is… I need two more people.

The letters confuse me.

Dad sends them a lot. Mom and I always get one at the same time. If he sends one to Mom, I know there's an envelope with my name on it too. Maybe he's just bored. I mean, he probably does have a lot of time to do nothing but write letters. Mom says he's lonely. I guess that's possible. I don't know. But the letters confuse me. Not a single one I've ever gotten from him says anything about anything important. He asks about school. He tells me he misses me, which is probably a lie. He tells me he loves me and thinks of me every day, which is probably true. He's probably scared to death that while he's in jail, I'm going to tell Mom about all the other stuff he's done she doesn't know about. That just goes to show how little he actually knows me. If he knew me at all, he'd know I can't tell anyone about it. I can't hardly even think about it. Sometimes he'll ask me if I need anything and that I can tell him, if I do. That makes me want to throw up.

None of what he says makes me want to write back. I don't really want to write back at all. But even though I kind of hate myself for it, sometimes I do write back. I don't say anything about anything either. It's easier to pretend he's a real dad when I can't see him. It's easier to pretend I have a dad at all. So sometimes I'll write back, tell him something about school and that we're doing okay. I never tell him I love him, though.

The last time I told my dad I loved him was when I was thirteen. He made me say it. He said he could stay all night. He was hurting me and so I said it. It's amazing what you'll say when you just want to be left alone. When you're so tired of being messed with that your brain just kind of shuts off. It's like you don't even know the words are coming out of your own mouth. You just say them because that's what you have to do in order to get him to go away. The fastest way to peace isn't to fight, it's to go along.

I wonder what he would really do if I told him about the kids at school. I wonder what he would think if I told him about the picture. He'd probably want to see it. I wonder if Mom told him about it. Sometimes at night, I pretend I have a real dad. I tell him about the kids at school and he marches up there, threatens them real good and makes them promise to keep their mouths shut about his daughter. Stands up for me. In my dreams, I have a dad who stands up for me.

I don't even know if I think dads like that actually exist at all anywhere on the planet.

So my letters never say "I love him." But they are nice anyway. They make everybody happy with me. Everybody, that is, except me. They make me feel guilty. They make me feel stupid. They make me feel like an ant in an ant hole. A good girl, a real one, wouldn't write pages of lies. That's what my letters are. I know why I write him back. But I get confused about his reasons. Why spend the time writing to me if he doesn't care? Why spend the time if I'm nothing but trash, like he said?

It isn't until I put my letter back in its envelope that I realize Mom's acting weird. She is just staring at the piece of paper. I know she's not reading it because her eyes aren't moving at all. One hand covers her mouth.

"Mom?" I ask cautiously.

She looks up from the paper and stares at me blankly. Then she blinks once, twice, and looks back down at the paper. I see her eyes scanning it this time. She's reading it again.

"Mom, what is it?" I ask, my voice rising just a little.

"Your dad.... He's.... he's coming home."

The world really can just stop.

It does for me. One minute, time is passing by. The next minute, I can't even hear myself breathing. I can't hear anything. Mom's lips are moving but all I can hear is what she's already said: ".he's coming home."

Fifteen months.

The judge, that judge, he promised me fifteen months. We were in the courtroom when he was sentenced and I distinctly remember him saying Dad would be eligible for parole in fifteen months. That's 457 days. It's only been five months, that's only 152 days. He's supposed to be away from me for another 305 days.

"How? How can – can he be released so early?" My voice doesn't sound like mine. It's hoarse. But Mom doesn't notice. She's trying to process it too.

"He got a judge to agree to it because of good behavior."

Good behavior. Good behavior?

He's being released because of good behavior. I say the phrase over and over in my head. It doesn't seem to make sense. How does a convicted felon get good behavior time? How can anyone who has broken the law and been arrested be given time for good behavior?

He wins.

The thought comes out of nowhere. I swear, nothing I do works out right. I turn around and make one of the most popular girls in school drop her tray. I don't have enough sense not to play a stupid game. I turn him in, and he gets good behavior time.

A knot grows in my stomach.

I feel sick.

"When? When is he coming home?" I ask.

"Monday morning."

Today is Wednesday.

Dad will be back here in four days. That means I might have a week before he'll come to my room again. I'm really sick to my stomach. I can't breathe. My face is getting hot and I'm feeling a little dizzy.

I mumble something, I'm not sure what, and run up the stairs to my room. I pace around the bedroom, swallowing past lump after lump in my throat.

He caught my eye.

When the cops came to our door, he looked up. I was standing at the top of the stairs and he looked up. He caught and held my eye. He didn't smile. He didn't shout goodbye. He didn't say anything. He just held my eye.

He knows.

He knows I called the cops.

He must.

There is no good way to describe fear. It's like a snake, coiling around your throat and then choking the life out of you. Fear is the knowledge, the very, very sure knowledge that you are trapped and, no matter what you do, you're not going to get away.

I jerk open my desk drawer, throw out all the junk, grab the razor and slice my skin. Blood pools but I don't even feel it. My heart is beating too fast. I slice again, just above the fresh cut, this time, a little deeper. It's spilling, it's spilling onto the carpet, the blood is, but I don't care. I have to make it stop. I have to make the throbbing in my heart stop.

I slash at my upper arm.

Not even the sight of the blood stops my heart from breaking. It's ripping in two. I can feel it. How stupid could I possibly be to think I could beat him at his own game? How stupid could I be for thinking it would be that easy to be away from him?

My arm starts to throb a little. My heart starts to slow down its erratic thumping. I toss the blade on the desk, and then reach under my bed for the towel. As I sit on the edge of the bed, holding the towel to my arm, I start to cry, rocking back and forth.

But my tears don't matter.

They've never mattered.

What I want is irrelevant. It always has been. I'm just a waste of space. Except when he's home and then I'm a toy. Nothing but a plastic Barbie doll for him to play with. He's going to be so mad at me. So very, very mad.

I'd rather die than be here.

That thought stops me short.

There's a gun here.

What if...

The panic starts to reside. I can breathe a little better. I sit real still, letting my head think hard. The answer is so simple and so easy it seems too hard to believe. *Death*. Death is the way out. If I'm not here, everybody will be happier. Mom because she won't have to put up with my attitude and crap all the time. The kids at school definitely would be happy. I couldn't get in anybody's way anymore. I wouldn't be taking up so much space anymore.

I wouldn't hurt anymore.

No more fear.

No more late night visits from Dad.

No more freak.

All at once, I know why I made the list of what I have. I know why I tried to think of who might could take care of what's important to me. I know why the gun is in the house. It all makes sense. This is the answer. This is what everyone wants.... All the kids at school want me gone. Mom may not know she wants it, but she'd be happier in the long run too. She wouldn't have to take care of me anymore, or worry about me. She'd be free.

And I'd be free too.
Four days. He'll be home in four days.
And I'll be gone.

I have this memory from when I was real little. I don't know how old I was but I know I was young. I'm standing in my grandmother's living room in a pink and white tutu. There is a pink flower headband holding my hair back and I am twirling. I am looking down at the floor and spinning around and around and around. I'm wearing ballet shoes, even though I did not take ballet lessons, and am putting on quite the show.

My grandmother and both my parents are in the room. They are clapping for me. They are happy. And I am happy. Because I am a beautiful ballerina. This memory is important to me because it is one of the only ones I've got when I was really happy. I haven't been happy like that in years. I haven't felt like twirling in years. No one has clapped or wanted to watch me in years. The thing about kids is, everybody likes them because they are cute. But once kids like me grow up, people stop caring about them because they aren't cute anymore. It's hard to be somebody when you're not a little kid and you're not a grown-up either.

It's hard to be somebody when you don't have anybody and when you do stupid stuff, like call the cops on your dad or flash your classmates. Sometimes I think about when I twirled for everybody. Sometimes I wish I could remember what it felt like being that young and innocent. Even though I know it was me twirling, even though I know it really did happen, it doesn't feel like it was me. I don't feel any connection to that girl who was twirling. I see her, but I don't know what she was thinking, I don't know what she felt. I don't know if she went to bed and dreamed of fairy princesses or if she went to bed and dreamed of failing. Maybe if I could just remember what it was like to be her... maybe if I could just remember what it felt like to be that innocent...

But I can't.

Because sometime after I twirled and twirled in my grandmother's living room, sometime after everyone clapped and loved me, a monster came. He didn't look like a monster; he had a happy face and smiled a lot. But he was a monster. And he attacked, he attacked me, he held me down, even when he was so heavy I couldn't breathe. Just like the sea witch Ursula took Ariel's voice, this monster took something away from me. Only it was worse than Ariel losing her voice because what I lost, I could never, ever get back.

He called me trash.

He called me bad names.

And I believed him. And so the words and the names, they were like weeds that grew up around my heart, choking me. The weeds choked the life out of the little girl I used to be. I lost her. Somewhere along the way, she slipped away and I wasn't her anymore.

And now....

Now, there's nothing in me that's like a little girl anymore. Now when I see myself in the mirror, I don't see a pretty little girl twirling. I see a waste of space. I see a pretender who wears a mask like a clown. I see scars. I see failure. I am a disgrace. I am ugly. I am useless. My body isn't special; it's just skin and bones. And fat. When I stand straight up in the shower and look down at my feet, I see a little of my stomach sticking out. It's not flat. Sometimes when he uses his mouth, Dad grabs hold of the fat of my stomach in his hand. It makes me feel fat. Because I am.

I am weird.

I am stupid. I've failed a test almost every day of school this week. At least, every day of school that I've actually gone to. And it's not over hard stuff. You have to be pretty stupid to fail that many tests.

I'm a bad daughter. I called the cops on my own dad. That should tell you the kind of kid I am. I remember once, when I was a kid, Dad was arrested for something and Mom started crying on the couch. I wanted to make her feel better but, I didn't. Instead, I just sat on the couch next to her and didn't say a single word. A good daughter would have at least tried to say something good. Sometimes when Dad would tell me to do something, like if he wanted me to use *my* mouth, I'd gag. And sometimes I wouldn't do what he wanted. Like he'd kiss me. Kissing is the worst. It's special and it just really bothered me. So sometimes I'd keep my mouth closed. He'd tell me to open it, but it was like my jaw just locked up tight. Once, I even bit him. I didn't mean to, but I thought I was going to get sick. His tongue was so big in my mouth and I felt my stomach rolling. I wasn't trying to bite him; I was just trying to close my mouth. I bit him, though. Who bites their dad? He said I just wanted attention. He said I was selfish.

As much as it sucks admitting it, he was right. I couldn't think about anybody else but me. I used to ask for stuff too. Whenever we would go to the bank, I'd beg to come in too. I didn't want to go through the drive-through, we actually had to go into the bank because, if we went into the bank, I could get a sucker. I *am* selfish.

I mean, even at school.

I just couldn't get it through my head that I'm not supposed to have friends. I kept trying to change that. I kept trying to have something I'm not meant to have. That's why I played the game, that's why I lifted my dress. I thought that if I did it, I would finally have friends.

That's the kind of loser I am.

I login to Facebook and scroll through the newsfeed. Everybody's talking about something exciting they are doing. Going on trips, going out on a date or to concerts, snapping a thousand pictures of themselves with all their friends. Every picture of one of my classmates with friends proves I'm just a nobody. These pictures, there's always like three or four girls together at least, laughing and hugging each other. I can't even get *one* person to take a picture with me.

Unless it's a bet, of course.

I don't deserve to be here. I don't deserve to even be alive. I haven't done anything good. I've thrown McDonald's plastic hamburger wrappers out of the car window before, even though that's littering. I don't know how to dance. I don't know how to talk to boys. I don't want to kiss anyone, even though almost all the girls in school can talk about nothing else. I'm not in any clubs outside of school and I can't even skate.

The more I think about the idea of dying, the more I'm sure it's the right thing to do. The only people who would notice are my mom and dad. I don't know what Dad would think, or say. Mom might cry but only because it would be a surprise. She wouldn't understand why. I'd have to tell her why somehow. But after a few days, she'd start to feel better. I wouldn't be here to worry about anymore. She wouldn't have to think about feeding me. She wouldn't have to work so hard because she wouldn't need as much money because she wouldn't have to feed me or buy me clothes or school supplies every fall. She wouldn't have to work so hard.

I wouldn't be a burden to her.

And it's not like things are going to get better. Things don't get better for people like me. Dads get out of jail when they have kids like me. Nobody ever wants to marry girls like me. And nobody wants to be friends with someone like me either. I mean, think about it. How many people do *you* know who look like me? And even if it's true that everybody has a soul mate… even if it's true that there's one person for everybody… there are seven million people on the earth… there's no way I'd ever find "the one."

But mostly…

Mostly, mostly, I think about the last few months that Dad has been in jail. I haven't been afraid of going to bed. I haven't woke up every half hour to make sure he's not sitting on the edge of my bed, watching me. For the last few months since he's been gone, I've actually slept a couple of nights all the way through. And deeply. When he's home, I don't really sleep, I just doze. I wake up a lot to make sure I'm still alone. But there's been a couple of nights since he's been gone where I've almost been late to school because of over-sleeping. I start shaking when I think about how, in four days, he'll be home again. I won't be able to sleep again.

I'll wake up every half hour. I'll open my eyes one time and he'll be there, sitting on the edge of the bed. Maybe he'll say he missed me and ask if I've missed him. I'll lie and nod because I'll be afraid he'll stay longer if I don't. He'll start touching me. He'll make me touch him. And the ants will come back, the ants that live inside my skin. I'll feel them crawling beneath the surface and start itching. That won't work so I'll get a knife and try to cut them out.

It won't work.

Nothing will work.

I'll probably go back to school every day because school will be better than being here. Especially if he knows I called the cops. My mind snaps back to the night he was arrested. They'd been fighting, my parents, the night before. When they knocked on the door, my heart leapt into my throat because I knew who it was. Then he turned and stared at me, just for a minute. He caught my eye.

What if knows?

What if he knows I called the cops?

Fear makes my throat muscles close.

When I was a baby, there was this guy. He paid Dad money to build him a house. A lot of money. Of course Dad never built the house and the guy got mad. Real mad. He had a warrant swore out for Dad, and we moved. But not fast enough. The cops caught up to us, arrested Dad. He spent time in jail for it. When he got out, the first thing he did was go back to that same town. The guy had a company, a real one, build him a house by then.

Dad set it on fire.

No one was home. Dad knew they were gone, he knew he was just burning the house. But still. He burned a man's house down.

Mom has a gun.

The only reason I can think of that she might own a gun is that she was scared. It tells you something, doesn't it, if somebody's so scared of her own husband that she buys a gun?

If Dad thinks I called the cops...

What would he do to me?

Even if he doesn't know anything about that, even if he has no idea I turned him in, I can't stand the thought of him anywhere near me again. I don't think I can do it. I don't think I can lay there anymore while he grunts over me.

It makes me feel like a wild animal. It makes me feel like dirt. It makes the ants crawl in my blood.

Maybe if there was a reason, it wouldn't have to be like this. Maybe if there was something good about me, something that might help turn things around one day. Maybe if I wasn't just taking up space, then, then it might be different.

I get out of the shower and stand in front of the mirror. I look at my hair that's turned dark by the water. I look at the freckles across the bridge of my nose, the ones that are sprinkled under my eyes. I stare at the cuts that mar my belly, my arms and my legs.

No.

There's nothing special about me. There's no reason to hope, not when the pain is so bad. Maybe that should fill me with sadness. But it doesn't. Instead, a little smile makes its way onto my face because, just like I know how to stop the bleeding when I've cut, I finally know how to make the real pain stop.

By the time I get dressed, Mom has left for work. That's good. I have something important to do. I start in the dresser drawer. I take everything out, every single shirt. But nothing. I put everything back quickly, and then look around the room, wondering where else she might hide something. I drop to my stomach on the floor, look under her bed.

Nothing.

I walk into the closet and stare up at the shelves. There are several decorative boxes. I grab one, shift through it. Nothing. I grab the second one, then the third and fourth. I feel frustrated. I know they're here. I stand in the middle of room and look around. It doesn't make sense to separate them. I go back to the dresser drawer and pull open the top one. I take all the clothes out again. I take the gun out and set it on top of the dresser. That's when I see it, the very small silver box laying in the back corner of the drawer. I don't know how I overlooked it before.

I pull it out and open it.

There they are.

I pick one up and hold its cone shaped, smooth body in my hand. I put it back down and breathe in real deep. Relief flows through every fiber of my body.

Bullets.

There is so much work to do. There is so little time. I only have three more days before Dad comes home. But I can't go away until everything is right. I can't go away until I know for sure that everything is done the way it should be. I've been thinking about everybody I know, about what I want them to know. I thought about leaving a letter to Derrick and Nick, the girls. But they wouldn't care. They would think it's funny, and they wouldn't get it. It wouldn't change who they are. So I don't want to waste time writing a letter for them. I don't really want to a write a letter at all. Maybe I won't. Maybe I won't write one. I'll just do it. The reasons why don't really matter when your whole life doesn't even matter.

That thought should make me sad.

A week ago, it probably would have, to think that my life doesn't matter. That probably would have made me sad a week ago. But not now. Actually, I don't feel very sad right now. It's like there was a huge rock sitting on my heart, a rock that was crushing everything. The rock was blocking my view. I couldn't see anything or feel anything but the pain. Now, having a plan has changed that. Having a plan has made the rock roll away. I can see light at the end of the tunnel now.

I've only got three days left.

I feel full of purpose. I'm a little worried about being able to get everything done in time but, other than that, I am happy.

I came to school today. I failed the test but it doesn't matter. I'm going to fail the year too. I didn't come to learn anything. I came to see Mrs. Simmons. I really like her. It's November now, almost Thanksgiving, and ever since I've been here, she's made me feel welcome. She's made me feel smart. It's really nice when someone tries so hard to make someone stupid feel good. It's really nice when someone goes out of her way to be nice to someone like me. I don't want her to think I didn't notice how nice she is to me. I want her to know that I care about her.

But she's not here today.

The one day I need her to be here, we've got a substitute instead. So instead I just sit in the desk and keep my eyes on the paper. I'm not really listening. I'm thinking about how smooth the bullets feel and how easy it is to pop them into the chamber. It's amazing to me how something so little can be so dangerous. I wonder how a bullet really works. Does it explode when it enters your body? I don't think it does because I've seen doctors on TV remove bullets from somebody's arm or leg. But maybe that's not really how it works. I don't think it'll hurt much. I mean, it'll be instant, it'll happen so fast I won't have time to feel anything at all.

And there will be no more late night visits from Dad.

There will be no more snotty high school girls or pee-brained boys laughing at me and calling me names.

There will be no more pain.

I don't know why I haven't thought of it before.

The substitute wants everybody to tell her our names. When it's my turn, I start to speak but here someone behind me whisper, "Her name's Slut."

I don't think the teacher heard but it makes my face turn red anyway. I say my real name and then I turn my head to see who's behind me.

Derrick.

He's laughing, like it's such big joke.

I look to the front again but, without thinking, I look back at that stupid face of his.

"Don't worry, Derrick, I'm going to go so far away from here that you'll never have to see me again."

He arched his brows and snickered. "Can't wait to see that day."

I don't know why, but that hurts my
feelings something awful. I look forward and
close my eyes. Used to, I'd have thought about
cutting. I'd imagine slicing open the skin,
watching the blood drip out. Not today. Today,
I think about bullets. I imagine how smooth
they are, and how warm they make my hand. I
picture them, the silver steel color cone-shape
escape.

It makes me feel a little better.

By the time school is out, I've made a list
in my head of what I have to do today. It will be
a fun thing, an easy thing. But an important one.
I walk home and go straight to Mom's bedroom.
I go into her bathroom and open up the closet.
On the bottom shelf there's a little powder box
decorated with flowers. I open it and see the
money she keeps hidden. I take out a hundred
dollars and then put the box back.

I don't like stealing from Mom, but I
have to do this and there's no other way to get
the money in three days. I stuff it into the
pockets of my jeans and walk out of the house.
We live close enough to the mall for me to walk.
It's not that far. Or so I think. It takes me an
hour but I finally make it to the mall. I'm really
thirsty from that long walk but I don't want to
spend the money on a Coke so I put it off until I
see a water fountain.

I drink for a long time, then look around
me. I'm sweating and I'm hot. And I'm mad at

myself for not knowing how far away this mall really is. I do not like the thought of having to walk back home. But I did it. All by myself. It proves to me something important. It proves to me that I can do important things, big things, with nobody's help.

I start downstairs.

I try on about five different outfits in the first two stores. What would you want to wear when you die? Would you want to be dressed real nice, since it would be a special occasion (you only die once), or would you want to be buried looking like you look every day? I can't decide. One minute, I want to look nice. Maybe it would be the only time I could ever look really pretty. Dead people don't look the same as living people. Their faces look... peaceful. I don't even know what that might feel like but I know that if there's ever a day when I don't feel scared, I want to look nice that day.

I try on a red dress. But that looks too much like the slut everybody at school thinks I am. I try on a white dress.... But that just doesn't look like me. I tried on a purple skirt with ruffles at the bottom and a baby doll white shirt. It's pretty... but it's not right. I move on to the upstairs shops.

Everything is so colorful.

That's what I think when I'm looking through the shops. I see lots of things in white and pink and green. I don't see much in black and even less in brown. See, I don't really want to dress in black. It seems depressing. And this is *not* going to be a sad day. I'm not going to be hurting anymore. I'm not going to be used anymore, or made fun of. What's sad about that? So, even though I love the color black and have worn it almost exclusively lately, I don't really want to die in that color.

Brown is okay, though.

Except, I can't find anything really nice in the color brown.

I go into a new shop I've never been in before. And the first thing I see is this beautiful satin A-line dress the color of milk chocolate. Around its waist is a cream colored satin bow. I think of the satin dress I wore to the dance with Dad and how pretty I felt in satin. It was one of the only times in my life I felt pretty in a dress. And the color is perfect. It's not depressing black and it's not bright pink.

It's warm.

I grab a size eight and head to the dressing room, my heart beating in my chest. I pray for this dress to work right, to be as pretty on me as it is on the hanger. I know before I ever zip it up that I'm going to love it. I can tell by the way it hugs my upper waist and then flows out freely at the bottom. I turn around to look in the mirror. I've always heard that girls cry when they find the perfect wedding dress, that there's something about seeing yourself in a dress that means something. I never understood it... until right now. Now, looking in the mirror at this dress, I understand. I picture myself lying on the floor in it, a pool blood under my head, my eyes closed, and my face peaceful. My body clad in satin that slides over my broken skin.

I buy the dress.

And I still have money left so I think about what else I will need. I go into a shoe shop and pick out a pair of brown high heels. Not because I will need them, but because I don't want to be buried barefooted. After buying the shoes, I'm getting tired of shopping. And I still have a long walk home.

Mom will be home from work soon and will wonder where I'm at if I'm gone too long.

I celebrate my perfect purchases by stopping at the food court and getting a McDonald's hamburger. Then I walk out of the mall with my bag on my arm and a smile on my face.

***** ***** *****

I'm almost done with the chores for the day. I've almost done everything I need to do today. I've almost crossed everything off my list.

Except this.

Sitting on my bed, I've got a couple music CDs spread out in front of me and my iPod. I've got my rock collection that I've loved since I was a kid beside me. A couple posters I've always liked. The pearl necklace. My diary.

I have to give these away. I want to give them away. I don't need them anymore, but I want to know who has them. I don't want Mom to have to go through a bunch of stuff. That would just be hard for her to do. I want it to already be gone so that maybe this whole thing will be a little easier for her. I haven't really let myself think about what she'll feel or think when she finds out I'm gone. I don't want to hurt her.

The problem is, I don't know many people who I trust with any of this stuff. I don't want it to go to just anybody. I write down names of people I know on one side of the paper and then the list of things I want to give away on the other side of the paper. I draw lines to match the things with the people. It takes a long time but I finally have it all figured out, except the necklace and the rock collection.

I might give the necklace back to Mom. That way it would still be in the family. I know she would take really good care of it. But I love that pearl necklace. And I waited so long for it. I just don't want to give it up.

I don't want to make the wrong decision. So I decide to sleep on it. I put the list away, and the rocks. I turn my light out and try to sleep. But I can't. I toss back and forth. When I close my eyes, I dream in nightmares. I find myself holding my breath like I always did when Dad came. You can hold your body so tight you're sure one wrong move will break it.

That was the worst nightmare I ever had.

The one where I was laying on a bed. Just me. I was stretched out, with my arms straight as boards by my sides and my toes pointed at the far wall. Nobody was touching me. Nothing was on top of me. But I felt this terrible pulling sensation. I could feel the skin stretching in my hands and my legs. I cried out, in the dream, screamed for somebody to help me. But the skin, it just kept stretching. My belly started stretching and the muscles in my forehead and nose, cheeks too, until finally the skin on the backs of my hands tore, ripped. Then my legs started breaking. My face. I was breaking, cracking, everywhere. I was being broken alive.

I always wake up from that nightmare drenched in tears and shaking. Instead of wanting to cut then, I rub my arms and the hands instead. I rub my cheeks and my legs. I run into the bathroom to make sure I'm not really broken somewhere. Only when I've checked in the mirror, only when I'm seen with my own two eyes that my body is not broken, can I go to sleep.

I'm scared of having the nightmare tonight. I'm scared of dreaming. They say that sleep is how your body processes what happens to you during the daytime. Maybe that's why sleep is my enemy. Who could ever really process all the stuff that's happened to me?

The worst part is...

You really can break. Just like the music box I had when I was little, the one that got cracked. People can break too. Maybe not like in my dream but they can break on the inside. A person isn't supposed to be a super hero, she can only handle so much before her brain splinters in two. The heart can break, you can actually feel it do so, and then your dreams break. And when your dreams break, your hope breaks. And when your hope breaks... when your hope breaks, then you don't have a reason to be brave anymore, you don't have a reason to keep trying.

That's what's happened to me.

I'm broken.

And when something is broken, it is trash.

***** ***** ******

Two more days.

There's this girl in science class.

We don't talk, ever.

But she's kind of like me. She's not really popular. Everybody kind of whispers about her because she's never made a single grade that's not an A. Ever. She's a genius. Which you'd think is a good thing. And it might be... except when you're in school. In school, being a genius is stupid because it makes everybody jealous of you.

The thing is, she's nice.

She's normal.

And I can't help but think that, since she likes science, maybe she would be a good person to give my rock collection to. It doesn't take long for me to see that no, no that's not the case. I can't give her my rock collection. She's good at science, but I don't think she really *likes* science. She isn't smiling, she doesn't even volunteer to answer the questions like she does in History. I can't give my rocks to somebody who isn't going to like them.

So they stay in my backpack.

When the bell rings, I go to Mrs. Simmons' class. She's back! I feel really happy to see her. I sit down in the desk and rip a piece of paper out of my notebook.

Mrs. Simmons,

Thanks for always being so awesome. I'll miss having your class.

I wait til the end of class. Then I swallow past the lump in my throat, walk up to her desk and hold out the note. She smiles at me, takes the note and gives me a hug. Nobody ever gives me hugs. She really is awesome. And now she knows I care about her.

The only thing I haven't given away is the rock collection. It's weighing my book pack down. I skip my last class of the day, History. I walk out of the school building and head home. I don't mean to, but I end up at the park.

There's a mom and two little kids already there. They are playing on the swings. I go to the swings. I push my feet, thinking about how Nick and I did that. I hear a little girl call for her mom's attention, and I glance up.

The little girl is pointing to a rock.

"I found a big one! Can I bring it over?"

"Yeah... Be careful now."

The little girl is about seven years old. She seems to be bright. She was very excited about the rock she'd found. She held it up, calling for her mom to look.

"This one's an airplane!" She said.

I smiled.

That's when I knew.

I reached down, took the bag of rocks out of my backpack. Then I walked up to the little girl.

"Hi. My name is Taya. What's yours?"

"Hannah."

"I used to do that, tell stories about rocks."

"You did?"

I nod. Then I hold out the little bag of rocks. "Yeah. I kept all my rocks too. You wanna see?" Hannah and I looked through several of my hundred or so rocks. She loved the oval ones. Like me. We play with the rocks until Hannah's mom calls for her to come.

"Hey, Hannah, wait," I say.

My voice gets stuck in my throat.

I look at all the rocks. There's at least a hundred of them. Each of them has a story. I love these rocks, the ones I've found from every state in the United States.

"These rocks.... I collected them when I was a kid. But I don't need them anymore. Would you like to keep them?"

"Keep them? Like them be mine?"

I nod.

"Okay!"

I stay at the park a long time. The sun is starting to set when I finally get up. It is hard to walk away without the rocks. My backpack feels lighter now. Freer.

And so does my heart.

One more day. He's being released tomorrow sometime. Mom's not even up yet. But I've been up all night. Thinking about today. There's something I just have to do. It's the biggest thing on my list. And the scariest. I just don't want to do it if I don't have to. If there's a chance that....

You know, the thing that gets me about Cinderella is that she kept wishing. She kept dreaming even when it seemed like nothing would ever go her way. She never gave up hope. Cinderella never stopped caring. I know something Cinderella didn't know. I know that caring makes no difference. You can care about something a whole lot and it still won't change the way it is. But still choosing to make wishes and dream even when you have never won in your whole life... that's true courage.

It's the reason Cinderella is my favorite princess. Not because she's the prettiest. Not because she has the greatest story. But because she never quit. I admire her because of that.

And a part of me wishes I could be like her. If I could find just a small reason to hope that things will be different this time, if I had a reason to believe there was something more to look forward to than... than what there has been in the past... then I might not have to do it. I might not have to die. But I'm not Cinderella. I can't just *hope* it will be different. I have to *know* it will be.

This is the only way I will know for sure.

I hope to know before tomorrow, before he comes home, because I can't go through even one more night of it. If I smell him one more time, if I feel his hairy legs against my smooth skin one more time, I'll burst. I won't be able to grind my teeth and lock my jaw closed. I won't be able to wake up and pretend the bugs aren't there. It would kill me. And I don't want him to do that. If I'm going to die, I want to do it.

I'm not supposed to.

You're supposed to be sixteen before you can visit the prison without an adult with you. But I'm going anyway, and I'm going to figure out a way to make the guards let me in. I have to see him.

Visiting hours start at ten on Saturdays. Mom won't think it's weird if I leave the house for awhile but I can't go until after she gets up. She'll think I'm going to the park again. I've been going there a lot lately. I feel like I'm sitting on pins and needles waiting for her to get up. I keep looking at the clock but it doesn't look like it's moving at all. I get dressed but then change the outfit three times. I don't want to get dressed up for him. He might think the wrong thing. But I don't want to look too casual, either, because this is an important day.

Finally, just as I finish dressing in a pair of dark jeans and a light purple t-shirt, I hear the water start in Mom's bathroom. She's up. She's going to be busy today. She'll clean and clean. She'll make the whole house shine. I know because that's what she always does. It always makes me feel weird, like we're getting the house ready for visitors when we're really getting it nice for Dad. The weird part is that that's what he's felt like for a long time: a visitor. He never tries to tell me what to do. I don't remember a single time that he ever helped me with my homework or came to a parent-teacher conference. He comes and he goes too, just like a visitor. So I guess it makes sense for Mom to try and make the house look cleaner than it usually does for him.

I wait.

I take deep breaths, sit on my hands and wait. I wait for her to get out of the bath and then I wait until I hear her downstairs. I don't want her to think something's up, so I wait a little longer. Finally, when I hear the radio playing downstairs, I think it's safe, and I leave my room. I run downstairs and into the kitchen.

I don't want her to think anything's different, so I take time to eat a Pop Tart. Finally, it's time. I tell her I'll be back in awhile and I give her a kiss. She's got her hair pulled back into a ponytail. She doesn't look much older than me.

I walk to school.

I sit down outside, near the front doors, and take my phone out of my pocket and the slip of paper I'd written down the number to the cab company too. I call them. It will cost me fifteen dollars to get from school to the prison and another fifteen dollars to get back to the school. But it's thirty dollars I have to spend.

I think about Dad while I sit outside school. I picture his smiling face, the nose that looks like mine. He probably thinks I hate him. But I don't. I don't hate him at all. I'm afraid of him, that's all. If he would just give me a reason not to be scared of him, then we could get along and everything would be okay. Maybe he will. Mom's always told me that he loves me, in his own way. He says he loves me too. He says I'm one of the best girls he's ever known. And he tells me I'm pretty sometimes too. If he loves me, if that's true, then maybe I just need to talk to him, maybe I just need to tell him I can't take it anymore. Ask him to promise me he'll stop.

I've got the pearls in my pocket. They are a family heirloom. Maybe they will bring me luck. I pat the outside of my pocket and take a deep breath, feeling the wind rush over my face.

The taxi cab driver is nuts. He really can't drive at all. He swerves and almost kills us by not really stopping at, like, five stop signs. He drives like he's on a racetrack. The good news is that, since he drives so freaking fast, it only cost me thirteen dollars and twelve cents instead of the fifteen they told me over the phone. The other good thing is that I was too busy screaming for him to slow down to really think about Dad at all during the ride. I'm very happy to get out of the cab.

But when I see the long building, with the tall barbed wire fence surrounding it, I get nervous again. What if this doesn't turn out okay? What if he gets mad at me for coming? I'm going to have to lie just to get in the front door. What if he gets mad at me for that? What if he tells Mom? But worst of all, what if he says no? What if I leave here knowing for sure he's never going to stop? I try to tell myself that, if that happens, it's okay. I'll just go through with the plan. But something about that thought hurts. Not the killing myself part, but the idea that he might not want to stop.

I am late. It is after ten, it's ten twenty. So there's not a line anymore. Everyone was here on time and is already inside. I can still go in, but first I have to sign the visitor's log.

"Do you have an ID?" The cop at the desk asks

I swallow past the lump in my throat, remind myself I have to act like I've done this before. And I have. Just not by myself. I pull out my school ID card and hand it to her.

She squints. "A driver's license?"

I shake my head. "Not yet. I've just turned sixteen."

She takes the card and looks at the list. My name is on the approved visitor's list. As long as she doesn't check my birthdate, we're good. She has better things to do. She shrugs and gives a nod. "Come on through," she says. I walk through the metal detector and am then waved into a side room. A female cop waves a wand over me, between my legs and under my arms. Makes me open my mouth and take off my shoes. My heart leaps into my throat. This, this searching, is the worst.

I'm clear.

I pull the pearls out of my pocket and grip them in my hand. I am so nervous I feel sweat run from under my arms. My heart is racing a mile a minute. I walk into the wide open room and see countless tables. Men in orange sit talking to people who love them. Dad didn't know I was coming, so he hasn't had time to be escorted down here yet. I find a table and sit. The noise is loud around me with chatter. It makes it hard to concentrate. Maybe I shouldn't have done this. Maybe I shouldn't have come. What if he knows I called the cops? What would he do?

The nerves turn to outright fear when I see him walk through the door. He's in the orange jumpsuit like the other men here. He's walking like he owns the place. He says hi to a couple men and looks around. He's looking for Mom. He doesn't know it's me here instead. I think about hiding. But then I don't. There's nowhere to hide.

He spots me finally and I see surprise flash over his face. Then he smiles.

"Hey, you," he says when he gets closer. He reaches out to hug me. He never does that. I could easily step away. But I don't. I let him hug me. If he'll try to move on, I will too. I smile and we sit down.

"How'd you get in here?" he asks.

"I told them I was sixteen."

"And they didn't check it?"

I shake my head.

"Wow."

He leans back, watches me for a minute, then says, "Something important must be on your mind for you to come out here. How'd you get here?"

"I walked to the school and then called a cab."

"Does your mama know you're here?"

I shake my head.

"Where does she think you're at?"

"I didn't tell her anywhere. I---I go to the park a lot. She probably thinks I'm there. I—I shouldn't stay long though, so she don't get worried."

He nods once, slowly. Then his eyes narrow. "So…"

I shrug, look down at my hands. The pears are still clutched in them. I move my hands into my lap to keep him from seeing that they are shaking. Dad is so calm. When you're sitting in front of him, you feel like you're next to the President or somebody that's just as important.

My stomach rolls, churning.

I don't think he knows I turned him in.

If he did, he wouldn't be acting nice to me right now. He even hugged me. So that's a good sign. It's a good thing he doesn't know. That's what I think when he shifts his feet.

"What's your on your mind, darling?" His voice can be as smooth as honey when he wants it to be. He calls me darling a lot. Mom says he started when I was a baby. I just know I don't like it. It makes me feel like something bad coming from him. But I am trying really hard to focus only on what's important. And pet names are not important.

"I just—I just wanted to come see you. I—I thought it might be good for us to talk before you come home."

He arches his eyebrows, tips his head. "Yeah? Talk about what?"

I shrug, clench the pearls tighter. "I was—I was thinking. I was thinking about how things might could change at home."

His eyes narrow.

"I mean, I don't think I've ever told you before, not like this, but it really makes me feel bad. You know, when you come to my room."

"I don't know what you're talking about." His voice is still smooth, calm. But his eyes are narrowed with confusion. I can't seem to look at his face for longer than a few seconds. My cheeks are on fire; my stomach feels like it's going to be sick any minute now. My heart is in my throat. Hope... that's what it feels like to have hope. When you can't breathe and you can't hear anything around you, when the only thing in the whole world that matters is the next sentence... that's hope. I don't want to let it go.

"I mean—"I look around and then lean closer to him. "When you, you know, kiss me and stuff."

"I'm not supposed to kiss you? I thought that's what dads do."

I don't know if he's serious or not. I can't tell. And, for all I know, that's exactly what dads do. I don't know what other girls' dads do at night. But I'm not stupid either. If he was supposed to, then it would be okay for Mom to know about it. Mom can never know. He made that very clear when I was nine years old.

I shake my head.

"Dad...." I say, and my voice sounds sad even to my own ears.

He takes a deep breath and looks around him. Then he looks back at me. He nods slowly.

"So you don't want me to come up to your room, is that what you're saying?"

I nod.

I hold my breath.

He looks away from me for awhile and then smiles. "Okay. That's fine. I won't."

I blink. I don't know what to think about that. That was just too easy. But he looks sincere. My eyes dart from his eyes to his smile and then back down to my lap.

"And you won't kiss me?" I say quietly. "Or, you know, touch me?"

"I don't know what you mean by that but no, if you don't want a kiss, I mean, you're old enough to decide that. No problem."

Silence.

I don't even know what to say.

My whole world feels like it's been turned upside down. This was not what I expected at all. We sit there, in silence, for a few minutes. I don't know what else to say. I nod finally. "Oh. Okay. Good."

He shifts his foot again, looks away. When he looks back, I see a glint in his eyes that wasn't there a second before. He puts his elbows on the table and leans in, closer to me.

"Anything else?" He asks.

I shake my head. "N—no. I—I just wanted to see if it would be okay if I was—you know, left alone."

He nods once, slowly. "Sure it is."

I hear his name called, see a tall man slap his back. Dad turns around and starts talking to the guy. I don't hear it. I just hear Dad saying he won't come to my room anymore. Shock is making my bones feel weird. Finally, I stand up. I'm done. I want to go home now. I have to think.

That's when the guy standing behind Dad says, "I finally get to see this hot girlfriend of yours in person, say. She's even prettier than the picture you showed us." He elbows Dad. "Looks like she could be your daughter, old man."

Hot girlfriend?

Looks like?

My stomach, it drops to my feet. My face floods with heat again. I don't hear anything Dad says, all I hear is that he's been telling these other prisoners that I'm his girlfriend.

"I—I'm not his girlfriend. I am his daughter." My voice is wooden. Dad laughs, making it seem like I'm telling a joke. The guy laughs too. Prisoners stick together, I guess.

I don't smile.

Dad says he'll catch him later and the guy leaves. I stand up.

"Sit down." Dad's voice is hard as stone now.

I remind myself he is still in jail.

There are cops here. Everywhere.

I don't have to do what he says.

I shake my head. "I'm going home."

Dad takes a deep breath. "That's alright, you do that. Mom'll be worried about you. I'll be home tomorrow, and we'll talk tomorrow night. Maybe at bedtime."

"I won't be there." I say quietly.

Dad smiles. "See you then, Taya." He leans over, kisses my forehead, stands and walks away.

I don't cry.

But my jaw, it's locked shut. If I relax it, tears will fall. It was a lie. He was going to let me walk out of here believing a lie. He never intended to stay out of my bedroom. His cronies think I'm his girlfriend. Arrow after sharp arrow pierces my heart. It feels like I'm being stabbed a thousand different ways. Nothing has ever hurt this bad.

I used to tell myself that maybe he didn't know, didn't know how much it hurt me. I used to tell myself that it was normal. And maybe it is. Maybe every little girl's dad kisses her. Maybe every little girl's dad comes to her bedroom after dark. I don't know. But I do know that most dads do not think of their daughters as their girlfriends.

That's why he always wants pictures of me when he's in jail. Not because he's proud of me. But because he needs pictures of his girlfriend to show everybody. I don't remember calling the cab. I don't remember how much the ride to the school cost, or paying for it. I don't remember walking home. I have no idea whether or not I ate, or anything Mom said to me. All I know is that I've been on this bed for a long time now. I'm curled up and have been staring at the wall for hours.

I don't feel anything.

I'm numb now.

My heart feels really heavy.

We'll talk tomorrow night. Maybe at bedtime.

That's what he said.

And that glint in his eye, the one I thought was proof he was sorry, it was a hard glint. I bet he does know I turned him, I bet he was just acting, like I do a lot. He was just pretending because he had to, because cops were watching. Nothing he said was true. I don't think anything he's ever told me my whole life has ever been true. And tomorrow, he's going to come home. He'll be happy and laughing. He'll hug and kiss Mom. He'll eat dinner with us and ask me about school. He'll ask who my friends are, because he really doesn't know anything about me at all. Night will come, he'll go to bed at the same time Mom does. I'll toss and turn, think about running away, maybe cut myself half a dozen times. I'll wait and wait and wait until my eyes can't take it anymore. They'll close and I'll be asleep when he comes in. I'll cry and try not to gag when I feel him come in me. I'll wonder if he broke something bad in me, if it's because of this one time I wouldn't be able to have kids. I'll wonder what it looks on the inside of me, which part is broken. There will be white noise in my head, so loud it hurts my ears. I'll wish and pray I could run from it.

Except wishes don't really come true.

It doesn't matter how much you care, you can't change the way things are.

Dreams are nothing but fairy tales and fairy tales aren't real.

He smiled when I told him I wasn't going to be here tomorrow. I wonder if he'll smile when he gets home and finds out I wasn't lying.

Friday, my last day of school, I saw something I never saw before. It was a sign in Biology. It said:

WE'RE HERE TO HELP

It gave a phone number too.

Suicide and abuse hotline. I wonder what they would do if I called and told them that today is the last day I'm going to be here. It's five fifteen in the morning. I've been staring at the clock for a long time. Mom's leaving to pick Dad up from the prison at twelve thirty. They'll be back around one thirty. What could someone on the other end of the phone say or do that would make me believe this isn't the only way? Have you ever wanted something so bad you'd do anything for it?

I feel like I'm trapped between two things I want. On the one hand, I'm really glad that, after today, I won't ever have to worry about another painful night or failing another test or being somebody's joke. Whatever comes after death, it's better than any of those things. I'm sure of it. But. On the other hand, it's hard when I think of Mom.

I slept with the pearls in my hand again. They make me feel like she's close to me because they were hers and she wore them. That necklace is the only thing that was on my list to give away that I haven't yet. I was going to just put them back in Mom's jewelry box but... I can't part with them. When I'm holding them, it's like I'm holding a little piece of everything family should be. Families should pass heirlooms down through the generations. Families should laugh with each other and eat dinner together and hug every day. Families should know something about each other, something important.

When I think of Mom, I think of baking in the kitchen. She has always let me help in the kitchen. She would pull a chair over to the stove and let me climb up on it so I could stir the pancake mix and water together. She would let me put the cookie dough on the pan in whatever weird way I wanted to. I used to try and arrange them in pictures. When I think of Mom, I think of how she taught me draw a five pointed star.

We were driving in the car and I was bored. She got some paper and asked me if I wanted her to show me how to draw a star. Hers looked so straight and pretty. Mine were always a little bit crooked but Mom liked mine the best: she said they looked like they were dancing.

When I think of Mom, I think of that last time we went shopping for clothes. We got into a fight because I wanted a t-shirt with a skull on it and she didn't want me to have it. I wish I'd never seen that shirt. I wish I'd just chosen something else. It was just a silly shirt. But I didn't know. I didn't know this was how it was going to end.

When I think of Mom, I think of her hugs. They are warm and she always holds on a little longer than normal people would. When I think of Mom, I think of how hard she's been working lately. She's almost never home anymore. She hasn't cooked or baked in ages. But that's because she's had to. She's had to work hard so I could have a roof over my head and food in my belly. She's never complained. She's never asked me why I was hungry.

When I think of never seeing Mom again, I get a little sad. I miss her already. I hope she will know that. I hope she'll know how much I love her. I need to tell her that today before she goes to get Dad. I'll make sure I hug her real tight and tell her how much I love her. Mom makes me wish I was stronger, she makes me wish there was some other way. Any other way.

I used my phone to take a picture of the Abuse Suicide Hotline poster. I don't know why, but I did. I roll over to my side, grab my phone from the night table and find it on the camera roll.

ABUSE SUICIDE PREVENTION HOTLINE CALL 24/7 1-800-SUICIDE WE'RE HERE TO HELP!

All I have to do is tap on the blue-linked number and my phone will call it. I don't know I'm going to click on the number before I do it.

All of a sudden, my phone says, "Calling" and I swallow past my fear. Cinderella would talk to these people.

"Abuse and Suicide Prevention Hotline, my name is Wes, what's your name?"

I freak out and push "End Call" four times. The line goes dead. Wes is a stranger. He doesn't know me. Whatever he would tell me is the same thing he'll tell the next caller and the one after that and the one after that. It wouldn't be true; it would just be nice to hear.

There is no help for me.

I go back to the camera roll on my phone, delete the picture with the number on it. I don't need it. I picture the gun, loaded now, in Mom's drawer. I was going to bring it in my room but I was afraid of her noticing it wasn't there. It's hard not being able to touch it. Touching it reminds me that an end is close.

I pull the pearl necklace out from under my pillow and play with the pearls. It's an heirloom. It's been passed down from one woman to the next. I am supposed to give it to the daughter I will never have. Nobody would ever want me as her mother anyway. I am too selfish to be a mom. I play with the strand until my eyes feel really heavy. I don't mean to doze off but I wake up when I the water turn off in Mom's room.

She's awake.

All of a sudden, I'm wide awake. I jump out of bed, drop the pearls on the cover and walk downstairs. I want to be in the kitchen when Mom gets there. I can't believe I slept so late. It's okay, she's still getting dressed, and I have time.

I put the pot of coffee on and two pieces of bread in the toaster. Mom taught me a secret to cooking eggs so they don't stick to the pan. We don't cook them in the pan. We put them in a microwave bowl. You can cook three scrambled eggs that way in about two minutes. They stick to your bowls, but it's still easier than having to stand over the stove. And faster too. I have three eggs and the toast on a plate just as Mom walks in the kitchen.

I smile brightly.

"Hi."

"Well, hi, Sunshine. You're up early."

I shrug and hold out the plate of food. "I made you this. Coffee's almost done."

"You made me breakfast? Oh, you're so sweet, Taya, thank you." She takes the plate and sets it on the table, then gets a mug for her coffee. My own toast just popped up in the toaster so I grab them, and stir my eggs in the microwave. By the time Mom takes her first bite, I'm at the table too.

We are eating breakfast together.

Because we're family.

After a few bites, Mom looks at me and smiles. "So, you okay about today? Dad coming home and all?"

I shrug, nod, looking down at the food in front of me.

"I know I've been working a lot but you've been doing a great job holding down the fort for me. Now that Dad's back, I won't have to work so much. Maybe me and you can go back to doing more things together."

I swallow past the lump in my throat, blink back tears. I nod. "Sounds good."

"I'll help you with all that homework that's sitting on your desk too," she says, winking at me.

She's happy.

That's what I think in my head.

She's happy.

I don't care why. I just care that she's happy. I don't want to do anything to spoil that. So I smile back at her. When I was scared of a really big bumblebee one time, she killed it for me and then rocked me on her lap. She always made me hold her hand when we crossed the street. She put oil on my forehead and prayed for me. She put up with me being moody. She put up with me arguing with her over buying a dumb shirt. Even when she screamed and yelled, she did it because she was trying to get him to act right. She was fighting for me.

"We might have to stop at Wal-Mart on the way home and get a few things. I can't find a single razor in the house and he might need a few things too. So it might be a little while before we get home, but it shouldn't be after two."

Mom can't find a razor because I have them all. In my room. Very carefully, so she don't notice, I use one hand and pull the sleeves down, over my wrists, so there's no way she can see the cuts. I feel light headed and dizzy. But I blink back the tears and listen to her talk. When she's done, she starts to gather up her plate but I reach out, take it from her hand and stand.

"I'll get it," I said, walking to the sink.

Mom smiles. "You're being awfully helpful this morning, Taya."

I smile at her, put the dishes in the sink.

"All right, then. I'm going to go grab my shoes and my purse. You going to be alright here, or do you want to come with me?"

I shake my head. "I'll be fine. I'll be fine. Mom?"

She looks up from grabbing the keys off the counter. "Yeah?"

Trying to sound as normal as possible, I shrug and say, "Love you."

She smiles, walks forward and kisses my forehead. Then she gives me a hug. I smell her sweet perfume. It smells like flowers, just like it always has. I close my eyes, fight to keep the tears away.

"Love you too, sweetheart." She winks. "Be back after awhile."

And she's gone.

Just like that.

***** ***** *****

The chocolate satin dress is lying on the bed. The gun lies on top of it. I throw the razor away and then dot the fresh blood off my arm. Carving the word FREE into my arm took longer than I thought it would. The R was hard; I couldn't get it to look just right. And the blood kept smearing things up. But I finally got it. I carved it above "freak" so now it says "free freak." I like that better.

Mostly, I like that I'm going to be free.

I won't be a waste of space anymore.

I thought I would be really panicked right now. I thought a million thoughts would be going through my head. But I'm actually really calm. I know this is the way it has to be. I'm my Dad's girlfriend. That's how he sees me and as long as he sees me that way, nothing will change. If he does know I turned him in, things will just get worse. If he doesn't know I turned him in, they will stay like they've always been. Neither is okay.

I've never have a boyfriend. Not a good one anyway because everyone will know I'm nothing but a stupid freak. And even if someone did ask me out, the first time they saw my arms, they'd leave. It's hopeless. I accept that now.

I slip out of my pajamas and put on the satin chocolate dress. It slides across my jagged skin, making me feel pretty and whole. I go into the bathroom and fix my hair. I want it down. I spray it into place, so that it falls around my shoulders. I am glad it's not purple. Then I reach into the bathroom closet and pull out five towels. I put two on the bed, one on top of the other of where I'll lay. I put two on the floor by the edge of the bed. If the blood drips off the side of the bed, it will fall onto the towel there and not the carpet. I'm going to lay the last towel over my chest so that not as much blood will get on my satin dress.

I put my new shoes on and then I sit on the bed. For now, I put the towel beside me. I'm not ready just yet. Instead, I reach over and pick up the strand of pearls from the table. I want to hold them but I know that they will fall from my hand if I do. Dead people can't hold things. Not necklaces. Not memories. Not pain. I think about everyone I've ever known. So instead, I am wearing the necklace.

I don't mean to, but I start whispering things to myself.

My name is Taya Christine Cotner. I was born July 11, 1998. I am left handed. My favorite foods are soft tacos and chocolate. Peanut M&Ms are my favorite candy. My favorite animals are dogs because they are loyal. My favorite thing to do is listening to music. Pink is my favorite singer. Mom is my favorite person. My favorite color is blue. My favorite flowers are lilacs because they remind me of Mom's perfume. I am a freak. A stupid, fat one. I wear a size eight, not a two. I have dirty blonde hair and blue eyes. I have freckles over my nose. I have scars all over my body because I cut myself. I flashed my breasts at my whole school. I was a boy's bet and my Dad's girlfriend. I am fifteen years old.

When I run out of things to say, I sit still. I move my eyes over to the desk. My note, the one that explains everything, lays alone on it. The last pen I'll ever touch lies on top of the paper. I look at the clock. It's one fifteen. They should be home soon. I have said my last prayer. I have told Mom I love her. I can be free now.

I lie down, on my back, and stare at the ceiling. I spread the last towel over me, right up to my chin. If the blood splatters, maybe it will splatter on the towel. I use my left hand to pick up the gun. It is heavy. I close my eyes. I move my right hand up to my neck until I can wrap my fingers around the pearls of the necklace. I move the gun to my left temple for the first, and last, time.

The barrel touches my skin.

I didn't know it would be so cold.

I have to write this letter to you. If you're reading this, then it means you found me. I've put towels on the floor and have tried real hard to keep it as clean as I can. I know it was still shocking and probably scary to find me, though. I'm sorry about that. If I could do it so nobody would ever know what happened to me, I would. But I don't want anyone worrying about me, wondering where I am or anything like that. Mom needs to know I haven't run away; she needs to know what happened to me. So there was no way to avoid the mess.

Mom's the only one who has ever really loved me. And she's the only one I've ever really, really loved. If it weren't for her, I'd have done this a very long time ago.

Mom told me to be strong. She told me to have courage. But I can't anymore. Staying alive is too hard, it takes too much courage. You have to get up, hoping for a good day, but in

*your heart of hearts, you just know that it's
going to be a day just like every day before.
Mom told me to have courage. Staying alive is
brave because, if you're alive, you have to keep
trusting people. You have to trust them not to
hurt you. You have to trust them to tell you the
truth. You have to trust them to take care of you.
But nobody does that. Nobody tells the truth
anymore, nobody wants to take care of me and
I'm just not strong enough to take care of myself.
I don't want to. It hurts too much.*

       *I've thought of Mom a lot lately. Ever
since I realized there was no other way than this,
I been thinking about her. I remember when I
was a little girl how she'd tuck me in every
night. Sometimes when she thought I was
asleep, she would come in my room, put oil on
my forehead and pray. Sometimes she would
pray out loud. She always asked God to protect
me.*

       *I don't know what I think about God. It
would be nice to think I'm going to Heaven.
When I was a little girl, I remember walking
down the aisle at church in front of everybody to
get saved. A preacher, Brother James, put his
hand on my head, made me recite a prayer after*

him, and hugged me. He told me I was for sure going to Heaven. I was saved.

But that was before.

Before I got bad. I mean, I hadn't done anything too bad at that point. I really was a pretty good girl all my life up til then. I obeyed my mom and my dad. And I didn't try to get away with anything too stupid. I didn't say bad words just to say them or anything. I said my prayers ever night too. I don't think there would have been too many reasons to keep me out of Heaven then. But then I turned bad. Bad things started happening at nighttime, and I didn't say nothing about it. I mean, it wasn't that big a deal, it wasn't like I was being beat or nothing. I didn't have bruises on me. At least not any that anybody could see. It wasn't as bad as it could have been, but it made me feel weird. It kept me from having any friends.

And friends is what I've wanted most of my life.

I thought I had them one night. One night, I thought I was part of a group. I thought I fit in. We laughed. I thought we were having fun. Really, they were just laughing at me. But I didn't know that then. Once, I thought I had some friends. I thought I was normal. Maybe I thought that because I wanted friends so much. I wanted to fit in. I wanted them to like me. So I did stupid stuff, stupid stuff I knew I shouldn't have been doing.

And they laughed at me.

I just wanted someone to talk to me. I just wanted someone to care. Nobody did. I'm just a freak. It's all over me. I've got cuts all over me. Nobody else has cuts on them. But I do. Last week, I carved the word FREAK on my right arm. I carved it so deep it's there forever now. It's like a tattoo. There ain't no point in denying what you really are. If you are something, you might as well own it. And I am a freak. Everybody at school knows it. Dad knows it.

Anyway. I don't know if God is real anymore. I don't know how He can be. It seems like if He were, He wouldn't put up with all the crap that goes on down here. It seems like He would stop it right quick when good people got a shitty hand dealt them. The bullies are heroes, and their victims are freaks. Does that sound like something the God of the Bible would be ok with? I don't know. I hope Heaven is real, though. And, Mom, don't worry, I asked Him for forgiveness for what I done tonight, so, if there is a Heaven, maybe He'll let me in. I hope there is one. Even if there ain't, though, or even if I go to Hell for what I'm doing, it's better than being hated or ignored here every day and messed with every night. And, with Dad coming home, this is the only way for me to be free.

I'm not doing this just because I'm bored. Or because I want attention. Or maybe I am. Maybe that's right, what they say about my kind. Maybe that is what we want, after all. I mean, if I had a real friend, even just one, maybe I would have a good reason not to do it. But I don't think it's because I want attention. Mom always said, "You only fight after you've tried every other way." I've tried everything. I've tried so hard. Nothing has worked. So this has to.

I'm doing it because my whole life is ruined. Nobody is ever going to see me as anything else anymore. I'm doing it because nobody is ever going to want to be my friend. I'm doing it because I can't get the bugs off of me, just like I can't get the scars off my arms. I'm doing it because I'm tired of waking up crying every night. I'm doing it because I'm tired of being scared of the dark. I'm doing it because, even if I turned eighteen and moved *out, nobody would ever love me if I didn't do it for him a lot, but even once is a lot, and I just can't handle it. It wouldn't be real love, because if I was tired one night or sick or just didn't feel like it, he wouldn't love me anymore either.*

Mom tells me to think of my future. She used to say that whenever I got sad, I should think about all the things I had to look forward to. Maybe I would have been a teacher. That's what I wanted to be, when I was little. I remember getting paper and writing addition and subtraction problems for my baby dolls to practice. I taught them. And I always did real good in school. Other kids, even the popular ones, would say tests were hard, but I never thought they were. I always made straight A's, so I think I could have made a good teacher.

Except that nobody would let me teach their kids, cause I've got scars on my arms and besides, I'd only mess it up like I messed up the game. I'd probably scare the kids, or pass somebody that couldn't even read. And the first time I ever saw a student bully another student, I'd fail him for the whole year even if he got real good grades on the tests. Yeah, I wouldn't make a good teacher after all. You have to be normal to have that kind of job. I'd probably end up a waitress or something like that. Besides, it don't matter. None of it matters if you're not loved and nobody loves me. Nick said he never loved me even a little, even though he told me he did. He was just lying, I guess. Cause everybody lies. And you can't be happy if nobody loves you. If you're just one of those people, like me, that is never going to get somebody to love you, then why bother being strong? What does it matter if you're brave, if nobody can stand being in the same room as you? He said I was ugly. He called me a freak, and everybody else did too. They said I was trash. And I know they're right because Dad thinks the same thing. He told me so. How could you ever possibly be good if your own dad thinks you're trash? Why even try? Mom used to sing me a song every night that said, "This little light of mine, I'm going to let it shine." But what are you supposed to do when you don't have a light at all?

    So you understand, right, why I have to do this? You understand that there really is no other way for me. I just wasn't ever as strong or as brave as everybody else. I was never really meant to be here. When Mom told Dad that she was pregnant with me, he cried, he was so sad.

That's what he told me. I was a mistake right from the start. I'm just trying to erase the mistake, that's all.

But I want Mom to know that it's not her fault. She did everything she could for me. She prayed. She made me go to school, even if I didn't want to. She used to play peek-a-boo with me when I was a baby, for crying out loud. I know because I saw the pictures of her doing it. And she wasn't afraid to hug me. I don't want her to think I don't remember all the good things she did for me. I don't want her to think none of those things matter to me, because they all do. She was a really good mother. She's probably the only one who will cry at my funeral. But I don't want her to. I don't even really want a funeral at all. What I wish is that I could just be burned and have my ashes thrown out to the sea. I don't like the idea of being in the ground. I've always been real scared of the dark. But it don't matter, I won't really be there, right?

One more thing has to be said.

Maybe no one knows, Dad. Maybe no one ever will. And maybe it wasn't that big a deal. I'm sure lots of kids have it worse than I ever did, just like you said. Maybe no one will ever know all the things you did, or made me do.

*Maybe no one will ever know all the things you
said, even when you didn't say anything at all.
Maybe no judge will ever send you to jail for it.
Maybe you'll live to be a very, very old man who
always drinks coffee without cream and two
things of sugar every morning.   Maybe you'll
never feel a need to tell anybody about me.
Maybe you'll forget all about it. I don't know.
No matter what else happens, though, I want you
to know one thing: you are the real reason I'm
dead. In fact, I really died a long time ago,
when I was just nine years old, didn't I? At
least, most of me did. And no matter what else
happens, now you'll know that, and maybe
you'll remember it every time I'm not there for
you to touch.*

> *So then.*
> *It's time.*
> *Mom, I love you. Please forgive me.*

> *Goodbye,*
> *Taya*

This little light of mine
I'm going to let it shine
This little light of mine
I'm going to let it shine
Let it shine, let it shine, let it shine

Hide it under a bushel, NO!
I'm going to let it shine
Hide it under a bushel, NO!
I'm going to let it shine,
Let it shine, let it shine, let it shine

Won't let Satan blow it out,
I'm going to let it shine
Won't let it Satan blow it out,
I'm going to let it shine
Let it shine, let it shine, let it shine

This little light of mine
I'm going to let it shine
This little light of mine
I'm going to let it shine
Let it shine, let it shine, let it shine

Sometimes it feels like there is no way out. Sometimes the pain is so intense it blocks the brain's ability to see the big picture. But there are others who share similar memories, and pain. There are others who truly understand; others who are waiting to hold us through the storm if we but ask.

The hotline phone number listed on the poster in this book is real. It is a United States National Suicide Prevention line for HOPE. If you feel like Taya, please call it now: 1-800-SUICIDE.

Maybe they won't have all the answers. Maybe they won't have the pixie dust that can make your nightmare go away.

But they might.

And, even if they don't, they will truly and sincerely listen about whatever you want to talk about, for however long you want to talk about it.

HOPE, Suicide Prevention:
1-800-SUICIDE

Self-Harm Prevention Hotline:
1-800-334-HELP

Alternately, anyone who wishes to may contact the author, Tiffini Johnson, directly at tiffini@tiffinijohnson.com

Author Interview

An interview with Tiffini Johnson about the new book, Broken, *her motivations and real life inspirations.*

Teenage suicide is a sensitive issue scarcely fictionalized like in *Broken*. What made you choose this as a topic?

I don't feel like I really choose the stories. I do know that it's a topic I considered on more than one occasion prior to writing *Broken*. Anyone who glances at the statistics behind teenage suicide would be scared. 1 in 6 high schoolers in the United States has seriously considered suicide, says a recent study by the Center for Disease Control and Prevention. 1 in 12 have attempted suicide. 13% of students aged 14-16 years of age admitted to having created a suicide plan. In research for this book, I interviewed several teenagers between 14-16 years of age. None of them seem particularly afraid of dying; in fact, death seems almost a logical alternative to suffering through bullying of either the traditional kind or through cyberspace. These are our teens. These are vulnerable, impressionable, precious beating hearts that feel they are being ignored, underappreciated or flat-out targeted by media stereotypes, their peers and/or their parents. They are hurting. And that hurts me.

Still, I am very much character-driven. I would not have been able to write this story without Taya.

Do you think Taya bought the bullying upon herself? Do you think she went too far in trying to gain the affection of her peers?

I think Taya was a normal fifteen-year-old. Even adults want the admiration and respect of our peers; teenagers need that affirmation. If they are denied peer relationships, they instinctively believe it's because they lack beauty or intelligence or athleticism—whatever it is they admire most in others. They internalize criticism from their peers in a way healthy adults simply don't. Right now, there is a challenge being circulated amongst teenagers called the Cinnamon Challenge. Basically, they are dared to gulp down a tablespoon of ground cinnamon without water in sixty seconds or less. But cinnamon is caustic and is not easily broken down. This challenge has resulted in dozens of hospitalizations over the past year. It can make the lungs collapse. And yet, there remain dozens of youtube videos depicting teens attempting the challenge. In these videos, you can hear their friends laughing as orange fie-like breath is expelled from the challenger's mouth. Many teens, particularly those with previously established low self-esteem, crave attention and praise from their peers more than they care about physical safety. So no, I don't think Taya went too far or bought the bullying upon herself. I think she reacted to bullying in a realistic and sadly common way.

How much of the book is autobiographical? Did you ever have a suicide plan?

No I did not. Like most hurting teenagers, I never consciously, truly wanted to die. But I wrote Last Wills and Testaments out almost nightly. And I deliberately denied myself food to the point where all I could think about *was* food. I took hair brushes and repeatedly hit my arms until bruises appeared. Like Taya, my father spent mine and my sister's childhoods running from the police for things like writing fraudulent checks and fraud. As a result, we were transient and attended multiple schools a year. Like Taya, I was sexually abused on and off from around age five to age sixteen and, also like Taya, I suffered silently. Like Taya, I am fortunate to have a mother who completely devoted herself to my sister and I, taught us how to pray and the importance of maintaining close immediate familial relationships. My mother anointed my forehead with oil and sang songs to me too. But unlike Taya, I was doubly blessed in the form of a younger sister. I am convinced that the two of them supported and taught me invaluable lessons on love and hope that helped me survive.

What made you finally break your silence and tell others about the abuse?"

My daughter. I was pregnant with my oldest and my father was about to be released from prison, just like Taya's dad. My father hadn't been home in about seven years but I was still very much afraid. I was unable to accept the idea that he would be allowed near my little girl. I wasn't strong enough to ask for help for myself but I was inspired to seek protection for my daughter. And that's an important thing to note for any teen who may feel like there's no hope. I wasn't particularly enthusiastically living life. I did not have a wellspring of hope or optimism. Indeed, I was scared to death of the idea of my dad living under the same room as I again. But love for someone else, an innocent little girl who depended on me for protection, lit a fuse in my heart. Being pregnant surprised me greatly—I had not planned it. No matter how mundane life seems, you never really know what tomorrow brings until you live it.

What does the title, *Broken*, mean to you?

There are some types of pain from which we never completely heal. If the only thing Taya had to combat was the bullying, I believe the power of her caring mother would have gotten her through it alive. Although wrong and tragic, the bullying wasn't really what caused Taya to do what she did. She could have healed from those wounds. But there were other scars, deeper ones, from which she could not simply walk away.

Taya self-harms by cutting. Why was this included in the book, and is it really that common?

It was included because that's what Taya's coping mechanism was. Good or bad, we all have one. Taya's was cutting. And it provided a way to shine a light on the issue. 50% of teens who are sexually abused will go on to self-harm. It is common. 1 in 5 girls self-harm; 1 in 7 boys. 90% of those who self-harm start doing so between the ages of 14 and 18. Taya chose cutting. Cutting does provide temporary relief from pain, it's like putting a Band-Aid on it. It works because, when you get physically hurt, whether it be through cutting or stumping your toe, your body releases endorphins. The job of endorphins is pain relief. So if you cut, then your body knows you're hurt and sends endorphins to help. Those endorphins temporarily make you feel a stronger sense of relief and control, thus the reason why self-harm is common. Eventually, however, your body will grow used to having so many endorphins around and they will stop being so effective.

You mentioned we all have coping mechanisms. What was yours?

Writing, thank God. I truly believe God gave me the gift of writing as a way of carrying me through violent storms. I couldn't talk about any of it, but I could write about it. And through writing, I healed. Also, volunteerism. I started volunteering at age 18 with several different organizations. Volunteerism changed my life by reminding me tangibly that we are all in need.

You drew and designed the cover. What is the story behind it?

I love the final cover but I initially struggled with choosing between two concepts. The other choice was no picture, just the title against the black cover. I would look at one, then look at the other, and throw my hands up in abject despair. Finally, I showed both versions to my sister and asked her to tell me in one word what each option made her think or feel. For the first choice, the stark black with nothing but the title, her word was "sadness." For the current version, the published one, her word was "fragile."

That sold me.

While Taya's story *is* sad, what I most want readers to think about is how fragile we all are and how little it takes to damage us emotionally. And the pearls added the human touch, the one tangible possession Taya was unable to give away, the one thing that could have been a reason to hope. It is perfect for the book.

Do you draw a lot?

No. Only for the books and only when I have to.

Did Taya ever do anything that surprised you?

Oh, absolutely. I had no idea she was capable of picking up a phone at all, much less arranging it. That surprised and delighted me. I also had no idea of the game or her behavior when I started the book. All of that is very atypical of my female characters, so it took me very much by surprise. To tell you the truth, Taya is the most complex character I've ever written. If I sound proud, it's because I am.

Was there a scene or line from the book that resonated with you, maybe crossed your mind more than once *after* it was already written?

Yes. After cutting once, Taya counted her scars and said that the scars were "proof I was hurt." That breaks my heart. No one should feel the need to justify or prove pain.

What do you hope people take away from your books?

I hope it lingers in their minds, makes them see someone they might otherwise have overlooked. I hope it makes them cognizant of the people around them and to the presence of hope.

***Broken* is out ten months after *Holding Home*. Does that mean we can look forward to another book in ten months?**

Hm, I don't know. I write very late at night and only when a character inspires a story. I will wait until I have another piercing character before starting a new novel. What I do know is that writing is in my blood; it's a part of who I am. In order to be completely happy or whole, my life has to include writing. So there will be another story---I just don't know when! Until then, I will write my blogs and speak in public and at schools. And I will continue to treat each day as precious, to think creatively and to teach my girls to live passionately.

Enjoy a preview of

Tiffini Johnson's

HOLDING HOME

The story of Michael and Mary
Beth, siblings trapped in a violent
home ripe with domestic abuse,
and the ultimate cost of secrets.

Available Now

Girls are stupid. Mary Beth can't even lay down without crying. And she has to have the light on too. She thinks there are monsters in the dark. One time, she ran into my room, jumped up on the bed with me and swore there was a monster downstairs that was killing Mama. And, I mean, there was a lot of noise. Like, I wasn't asleep either, even though I pretended she'd woke me up. There was a lot of screaming and stuff. I even heard something bang real hard against the wall. But it wasn't a monster. I told Mary Beth that it was the TV, that Mama and Daddy had it up too loud. Mary Beth's six, I thought she wouldn't know any different.

"I ain't stupid, Michael," she shot back. Maybe not, but she was a baby. I mean her whole body was shaking. I could feel it because she'd crowded real close to me. She knows that I can't stand crying, and won't let her in the bed if she does it, so she wasn't crying right now. But she was scared. I knewed she was. She had the cover over her head and she was begging me to go help Mama. "You gotta, Michael, you just gotta. The monster, he's killing her."

"Monsters ain't real, Mary Beth, it ain't a monster."

"It is so!" she yelled. If she was smart, she'd know better. She'd know that it was Daddy. And she'd know I couldn't do nothing bout it. But Mary Beth thinks I'm bigger than I really am. She thinks I'm a monster slayer. She thinks I can make it stop. Make the noise, the screaming, make it all stop. She thinks I ain't scared. And I'm not, not really. I just don't like doing it, is all. I just don't like seeing it. It's not about being scared. I mean, cops don't LIKE having to shoot people, no matter how bad they are, no matter how many times they seen crazy dudes do stupid things.

Real cops don't wanna shoot nobody, they wouldn't get all excited if somebody said, "hey, you can shoot holes through him right now." Real cops would think of other ways to get the job done first. Not because they were scared, but because shooting people is a bad thing. So I ain't scared to go help Mama, I just don't wanna do it. Like, part of me knows better than to get in the way. I been listening all night and, I mean, she DID ruin his best shirt. She said so herself.

The thing you gotta know about girls, though, is that they don't give up. And too, they make you feel real crappy if you can do something for them but don't. Mary Beth wasn't crying, but I'm starting to really wish her body would stop shaking. I roll away from her, pull the covers up to my chin and shut my eyes. If I'm real still, maybe she'll go to sleep. Maybe she'll go back to her room. The stupid noise is a little quieter right now. Maybe I won't have to get up after all. My eyes open. The quiet downstairs makes me nervous. Why is it so quiet? I stare at my window. The moon shoots rays of light through the curtains, and I can see three little stars. I think, "nobody out there has a clue." Sometimes, especially after nights like this one, I think the outside works like a TV show: the people aren't real, the houses aren't really real. It all looks so pretty. It's summer right now and so everything is so green and there's lots of flowers. It looks so colorful. It's so different, it feels like the only thing that's real is what's inside our house. Our ugly house. I think--

The scream that pierces the house is deafening. Mary Beth jumps behind me and starts crying again. Her legs bend up, her knees hitting me in the back. Her sobs make her shoulders shake, which makes the bed move. She's scared. And that was a loud scream. Mary Beth thinks Mama's dying. What if she is? What if I stay in this bed, and then find out she's dead in the morning? It would be my fault, cause I know how to stop it. I just don't wanna. But then I remember: a good cop don't want to shoot nobody but, when he's gotta, he will. The screams and shouts have started back again. Something just broke. Daddy's voice is loud. Mama's screams are loud, but not as loud as before. My stomach hurts cause I know I just gotta do it.

I throw the Batman covers off and stand up. My legs feel cold and I wish my red and blue fire truck shorts were pants. "Stay here," I tell Mary Beth. She doesn't come out from under the covers but I know she won't leave the room. She'll still be under the covers when I come back. The hardwood floor is cold under my feet. The shouts get louder when I get into the hallway.

"My only good shirt for work and you can't even wash it right! Are you color blind or something? How stupid can you be? Everybody knows you don't put a blue shirt in with the damned whites!" A scuffle. Mama is crying. I hear the sound of skin being pounded. I think I'm the only eight year old boy in school that knows what that sound is, but I could recognize it anywhere. I'm almost to the stairs.

"And what the hell kind of shirt is that you're wearing? Here I am, going to work and giving a lazy piece of shit my money to buy herself some clothes and she buys Dollar Store junk. What, trying to look poor so people will feel sorry for you? To hell with that. I bought it, give it back. If you want to look like a homeless whore, you'll do it without my money." Mama says she's sorry, says she won't forget again, but I hear more noises, ripping sounds. Another scream.

My heart is pounding like crazy. I put a hand on the staircase railing and look down. I can't see them yet, though. I tiptoe down a couple more stairs, closer and closer. I can feel a whirring noise in my head, getting louder and louder and louder. My legs get shaky. I wonder if the cops feel this way right before a shoot out. I walk down more steps, quiet as I can. I see Daddy first. He stands with his legs apart, looking like a statue near Mama. I can't see his face, only his back.

I see Mama next. Except she don't look like Mama. She looks like Mary Beth. She is on the floor, on her side, her legs curled up. She does not have a shirt on. She shakes like Mary Beth. I stand still on the stairs, my eyes wide. Daddy don't see me yet. Mama don't see me. I didn't see it until it came down without warning on Mama, the belt. I know what it looks like, even though I can't really see it right now. It has silver buckles. It is heavy too. I know that. Mama jerks. I do too. It makes me feel stupid, like Mama. She's on the floor. I mean, if she stood up, she could get away. I never understand why she don't get up.

When I jump, Daddy turns. He sees me. His face is red. His brown eyes are wide. His hair, dark, it needs a brushing. He looks strong. He is strong.

"Hey, Michael. D'ya mama wake you up? She ruined my work shirt. Gotta spend twenty dollars to buy a new one."

I say nothing. I look at Mama. Her blue eyes are swollen, the whole right side of her face is a green, black color.

She is not crying, but looks like she's about to. She has a black bra on but one of the cups is about to come down. I can see a few bones under the skin. The last time this happened, Daddy called her a rabbit. She does kind of look like one when she's all curled up on the floor.

Daddy leaned down and grabbed Mama by the hair. My eyes slide away but I hear him punch her. I wait for it. I know it's coming. So I wait for it.

"You wanna turn, my boy? You're man enough, right? Go head and tell 'er what she's done to you today. Show her what you think."

I thought about this as I came down the stairs, cause I knew it was the way to end it. I knew he'd ask. So I already thought about it. The trouble is.... She didn't really do anything wrong. She usually don't. Least not to me or Mary Beth. I mean, sometimes my bath water is a little cold, I guess. But she says that before you can really get mad at somebody for something, you should tell them what it is that isn't right. She says that's only fair, cause people cannot read minds and don't know something's wrong less you tell them. And I've never told Mama that she gets the bath water a bit cold. So I don't count that. If I don't count the bath water... Mama almost never does anything wrong. I mean, she plays with us... Even if she won't let me play that I'm shooting bad guys.

When I don't say nothing, Mama's eyes look up at me. They are swollen, and blue. She looks sad. But that makes me mad cause she's a grown up. If she don't like something, she should just change it. But she can't cause she's a girl. Stupid girls. I am quiet too long. Daddy kicks her in the stomach when she starts to sit up. Maybe that's why she don't stand up. Cause he won't let her. And good cops help those that can't help themselves, even if they are stupid sometimes.

"She didn't let me play shooting." My voice sounds hoarse, dry, quiet. My heart is pounding and I wonder if Mary

Beth really stays hidden under the covers. I hope so.

"You tellin me she won't let you be a boy? Trying to turn you into a sissy?" Daddy kicks her. She covers her face, but don't make a sound. That always feels weird to me. She screams until I come down. Then she never makes a sound. Maybe she screams for me. Maybe it's her way of asking me to come help her, help Mary Beth. That gives me courage. When Daddy holds out the belt for me, my hands and knees start shaking. I don't wanna. I don't wanna. She may be stupid, but I love her. If I don't, he will. Mary Beth won't stop shaking. I try to think about the twenty dollars Daddy is shouting about. I try to think about taking a bath in cool water. I squeeze my eyes shut, as hard as I can, and bring the belt down. I feel it hit skin. I know it hit her. I felt it vibrate. Daddy starts laughing, tells me to do it again. If I say no, he'll get mad. If I say no, he'll want to teach me to be a man. So I do it again. My ears are ringing, my hands are sweaty, my

heart is racing. I just want it to stop.
After the third time, my arms start
shaking, and I accidentally drop the belt.
I don't mean to, but I am crying. Mama is
crying. Daddy turns and walks away.
He's done.

      I can't look at Mama. The floor is a
mess. Broken pieces of a vase are
scattered everywhere. Blood, too.
Mama's blood. She moves a little. She
lifts her head, looks at me. She takes a
breath, but I swipe my eyes. I'm not
crying, it's just sweat, that's all. I don't
know what to say so I turn and run
upstairs. I'm almost to my room when I
see Daddy at the laundry room. He is
putting clothes, all white except for
Mama's black and red church dress, in the
washing machine. I race past him and
into my room. Mary Beth is still in my
bed, but not under the covers anymore.
Her wide eyes look like Mama's and
makes me look away from her. As I walk
to the bed, she says, "The monster's
stopped." I get into bed, roll away from
her and say nothing. Mary Beth climbs

out of the bed, her feet brushing my ankles as she climbs down. "Teddy's in my room," she says, then walks to the door. Before she leaves, though, she stops. "Michael?"

I don't answer.

"Thank you."

Then she's gone. I lay, staring out my window. My teeth are chattering. My hands hurt. I clench them into fists, then stuff them under the covers and between my knees. I don't want to shake, but I do. I don't know how long it is before I relax and my eyes close. I see a huge blood red monster. He's turned away from me, but his back is full of lumps and green boils. He is tall as a tree, and he's screaming. I can't hear what he's screaming though. There's a dog in front of him. The dog is cute. It's a white little puppy. It barks and the monster steps on it. It's not a dog anymore, just a pile of yellow goop. The monster jumps on the pile and starts roaring like a lion. All of a sudden, the monster turns towards me and I feel myself scream: the monster has my face.

My eyes pop open, I am breathing really fast. There is someone kneeling beside me. Someone small. A warm hand brushes the hair off my forehead. It feels nice. It calms me down, keeps my breathing from going crazy. It is still dark in the room but, through the shadows, I can see Mama's face. She smells nice. She always does. Like babies and flowers. I don't say anything. I close my eyes real quick, cause I don't want her to talk, and I don't want her to stop. She keeps brushing my hair back for awhile. Then she leans over and gives me a kiss on my forehead. She rests her cheek against my face for a minute. Her skin is warm and nice. She gives me another kiss and whispers, "I love you." I keep my eyes closed as she stands and walks out of the room, clicking the door shut behind her. I finally breathe.

It is hard being the hero.

Meet Tiffini

Once upon a time a blonde haired, blue eyed girl was born in Memphis, TN. She started writing when she was six and never stopped! By the time she graduated high school, she had written over 100 books, the longest of which was over 2000 handwritten pages long! Today, Tiffini has grown up but still believes in the power of stories and continues to write them from her home in Nashville, TN.

Tiffini is a mother to two little girls, Breathe and Alight, and spends her days with them playing pretend and believing in a world in which happily-ever-after is more than make believe.

She's an insomniac who stays awake into the wee hours of the night via the help of many Dr. Peppers. She's a teacher and an advocate for abused and neglected children: she travels to speak to school and churches and youth groups about her journey through abuse and how God saw her through.

Best of all, she is living happily ever after! To communicate with Tiffini, you can e-mail her at: tiffini@tiffinijohnson.com, visit her regular blog posts at storiesthatmatterblog.com or her website at tiffinijohnson.com. You can also snail mail her at:

Stories That Matter
4140 Pleasant Colony Dr.
Antioch, TN 37013

Made in the USA
Las Vegas, NV
14 August 2022

53235493R00173